First published in Great Britain in 1998
by Collins & Brown Limited
London House, Great Eastern Wharf
Parkgate Road, London SW11 4NQ

British Library Cataloguing-in-Publication Data:
A catalogue record for this book
is available from the British Library.

ISBN 1 85585 623 9 (hardback edition)
ISBN 1 85585 651 4 (paperback edition)

Editor: Stephanie Donaldson
Designer: David Fordham

Reproduction by Grafiscan, Italy
Printed in Hong Kong by Midas

BLUE & WHITE LIVING

STEPHANIE HOPPEN
FRITZ VON DER SCHULENBURG

COLLINS & BROWN

BLUE & WHITE LIVING

Contents

LEFT Shades and tones of blue and white are reflected as much in nature as they are in design, illustrated here in the turquoise waters of the Maldives and the azure blue of a swimming pool, the deep blues of the ocean and the hazy blue of the skies above Toronto and La Grande Montee.

BLUE, THE COLOUR OF EYES, THE SKY, THE SEA and of heaven, is probably everybody's favourite colour. It is also the only colour whose shades can be mixed together with an invariably happy result. Blue also co-ordinates beautifully with other colours – blue and white, blue and red, blue and yellow. In fact, it is one of the most popular colours used in our daily lives – 'Blue de Nimes' or blue denim is a universal favourite. China plates and crockery, bed and table linen, furnishing fabrics, wallpaper and Portuguese 'Azurelos' tiles have all favoured blue, whatever the age or style.

Blue represents elegance, simplicity and tranquillity. What other colour commands such enthusiasm, and for so long? In the art world, what painter has not had a 'blue' period – Picasso and Matisse are two of many. The greatest interior designers, past, present and to come, never tire of using blue, and all of them, at one time or another, have wanted to design a blue and white room. Blue has always featured in our own collection of furnishing fabrics. It is a timeless colour which can be used to great effect in *camaieu* (monochrome) or in combination with another colour.

This book is a wonderful idea and throughout these pages, you will discover a multitude of shades, uses and locations that Stephanie Hoppen has chosen or created with such great talent and we will always be grateful to her for having written this book. It is a beautiful testament to blue and white and will always be studied with pleasure.

Patrick Frey

MY LIFE IN BLUE & WHITE

Although I have always loved blue and white as a colour combination, I don't think I had any conception of how wonderful it was until about twelve years ago when I bought an enchanting house in Chelsea, London. The dining room of my late 18th-century home was to display all my blue and white china.

Over a period of one year, a rather special room evolved: the blue dining room that has appeared in almost every home magazine and book about dining rooms in the Western world. The centrepiece of the dining room is a marvellous 17th-century Dutch china cupboard. Its exterior is almost a silver white with shelves painted in a faded, distressed blue, signalling its aristocratic heritage. It was evidently meant to store and display all the porcelain and ceramics that would have been essential to any Dutch household. Before the cupboard was delivered, we painted and dragged the walls in the same blue as the cupboard shelves. When it arrived, the room began to look alive. I began filling every niche with my china and porcelain, and the plates that did not fit into the cupboard we hung on the walls.

LEFT I have set my table, a monastery table from Guinivere, for an elegant but relaxed lunch. The dinner plates and finger bowls date from the 19th century, the glasses and napkin rings are handblown by Antony Stern of Battersea and the vases are favourites from my collection, but shops like Habitat and Crate & Barrel offer similar crockery and I have always found flea markets to be good sources.

The room began to take shape, and I searched high and low for a fabric that would be the perfect blue for the room. I finally decided on a Fortuny fabric – and of course, one that had not been produced for simply ages. As there was no stock, we had to have it custom-made and this took some time. Yet when it came, we made so much with it. Along with a silk striped fabric by Bernard Thorpe, we created curtains, blinds, a cloth to cover a cheap chipboard round table, and chair seat covers.

By this stage the room was very blue and white, and I decided that I would continue, and make it obsessively blue and white – china for the table, glass, table cloths, pictures for the walls – everything. It became the most successful dining room I had ever had. People loved dining there and, evidently, everyone loved reading – and talking – about it. At the gallery, I still receive many calls enquiring about my blue and white room.

I have now turned my attention to the kitchen (illustrated opposite and on pages 62–63) where a floor-to-ceiling cupboard houses the items in daily use while a dresser contains more precious pieces. It is a very practical room and one that is in constant use. Here I entertain friends informally and I find the conversation so often turns to talk of blue and white. My friend Kate Dyson, whose kitchen dresser is photographed on page 11, also adores blue and white and has a comprehensive collection of blue and white china. My bedroom too, shown on pages 80–81, is hopelessly blue and white, but I can honestly say that I never tire of this combination.

Thus began the germ of an idea about a blue and white book. Not just about blue and white in the conventional sense, but all the shades from indigo through to Swedish blue; I wanted beautiful photographs to showcase fantastic ideas from all over the world. Along with details to show how each look was created, you can see how my favourite colours can act as subtle accents in a room, or study the collections of blue and white arranged to form a wonderfully eclectic style.

This book grew from my endless love affair with blue and white. Although I am almost constantly surrounded and inspired by my favourite colours, it appears that the charm of blue and white is quite inexhaustible.

I owe a big thank you to all those people who allowed me into their blue and white homes, all the fabric houses who let me use their fabrics and, in particular, Isabelle from Pierre Frey; Karen Howes who worked with me on long, hot days to find us what we wanted and never complained; and Julia Lowery at my gallery who found everything each time anyone lost something. And finally a big thank you to Fritz von der Schulenburg whose enthusiasm and taste are infectious. Working with a person who never tires or loses his humour is a delight.

I hope that when looking through this book you will be inspired to find a way to introduce the blue and white look into your own home. We may not live in castles, palaces or idyllic country retreats, but we can all enjoy the beauty of blue and white living

9

BLUE & WHITE CHINA

RIGHT

The top of the dresser, left to right

1. Deep blue English transfer printed ironstone platter with a fishing scene by Rogers, c. 1820.
2. Blue and white tureen lid, Swansea, chinoiserie pattern, c. 1790.
3. Blue and white teapot, Chinese, late 18th century.
4. English platter, Rogers, a later edition of the first platter on the left, c. 1840.
5. Stone china platter, Staffordshire, 1830s.
6. Chinese willow platter.

The top shelf, left to right

1. Masons ironstone china blue and white jug, c. 1820.
2. Pearlware charger, English, c. 1810.
3. English transfer printed plate, Henry Jetzen, bird pattern, by Thomas Dimmock.
4. Spode Jasmine pattern plate, impressed mark, early 19th century.
5. Early flow blue plate by Wood and Sons, Burslem, a view of Liverpool c. 1810.
6. New Spode repoduction of 1820s botanical pattern plate, one of Spode's most sought-after patterns, dating from the early 1800s.
7. Fairy Villas plate by Maddock and Seddon, Staffordshire, Burslem, 1840s. One of a series of romantic Chinese scenes.
8. Dutch blue and white Delft dish, c. 1770.
9. French blue and white enamel jug, c. 1920.

The centre shelf, left to right

1. British scenery by Booths, Tunstall, Staffs, miniature jug, c. 1900.
2. Yuan bird pattern plate by Encoch Wood and Sons. Another popular blue and white pattern, much copied over the years.
3. Booths dessert plate 1876–1883, Indian ornament pattern.
4. 19th-century willow pattern cup, c. 1810, maker unknown. Typical of porcelains made from 1770–1810 when Chinese patterns were fashionable. Willow pattern is the best known one.
5. Minton delft pattern plate, impressed and printed Minton, England, c. 1890–1910.
6. Victorian blue spongeware mug, c. 1850. Sponging is one of the most popular traditional methods of decorating pottery.
7. Village fisherman, pattern plate by J and W Handley and Co, c. 1825.
8. Royal Danish blue and white plate, c. 1920s. This is one of the most famous traditional patterns to be found in the beautiful and much-prized Copenhagen porcelain.
9. Copeland and Garrett transfer printed plate c. 1833, decorated with one of Byron's views – a series of illustrations from a popular book on Byron.
10. 'Death of the Bear' by Spode from their famous and rare Indian sporting service, made in 1812.

11. George V flow blue ale mug – a typical pub mug decorated with hops.
12. Rogers farm scene, with ruins in background, cows in foreground.
13. Blue and white floral transfer mug, maker unknown, 1840s.
14. John Stevenson and sons elephant pattern, a later copy of a 1780s transfer.
15. Blue and white spongeware mug 1850.
16. Rogers vine pattern, blue and white, 1784–1836.
17. Blue chinoiserie cup, English porcelain with gilded edge, c. 1810.
18. Miniature gravy boat, willow pattern, c. 1900.

The bottom shelf, left to right

1. Modern Spode blue and white rose mug, a copy of a famous 1825 pattern.
2. Blue and white Greek pattern pearlware plate with arcaded edge.
3. Spode breakfast cup, a new copy of an 1831 transfer.
4. 1880s Minton porcelain plate – oriental-style.
5. (front) Small sheet pattern pearlware saucer, c. 1800. (behind) Continental porcelain plate, late 19th century. The pattern is inspired by a famous Sevres design dating from the 18th century.
6. Early 19th-century chinoiserie saucer with gold edge, c. 1810.
7. Parian ware spotted jug – late 19th century – another type of blue and white.
8 & 9. Saucers, early 19th-century chinoiserie with gold bands.
10. Coalport blue and white milk jug.
11. Miniature teapot, early 19th-century, Worcester, England.
12. Wedgwood water lily pattern plate, 1822, showing the bold botanical designs, popular at the start of the 19th century.
13. Cornish ware mug.
14. Spode Greek pattern mug, 1806, pattern on new edition.

The front of the dresser, left to right

1. Blue and white jug, Caughley M mark.
2. Worcester tea pot and cover.
3. Hot water plate – grazing rabbits, maker unknown, 1820s, one of the most sought-after rare early transfer patterns.
4. Large blue and white jug, Chinese, late 18th century.
5. Castleford teapot, c. 1810, with sliding metal lid. Another version of blue and white.
6. Large late 18th-century blue and white Chinese bowl. Chinese influence formed the backbone of European porcelain design.
7. Enamel French butter dish. Yet another version of blue and white, dating from the 1920s.
8. Late 1830s Staffordshire jug, blue transfer onto blue body.
9. Miniature blue and white teapot by Meissen – a rare piece dating from the late 18th century and illustrating the best of Continental blue and white.
10. Wedgwood bowl, 1860, applied blue decoration onto creamware body.

ONE

THE WORLD OF
BLUE &
WHITE

LEFT The Sobha Niwas, Hall of Brilliance, situated on the third floor of the Chandra Mahal which forms part of the City Palace in Jaipur, India and where successive Maharajas entertained.

I HAVE HAD A LIFELONG LOVE AFFAIR WITH BLUE and white in its many variations, but it was not until I started work on this book that I realized the extent to which I shared this obsession with a large proportion of humanity from differing cultures and different times. The world over, there are wonderful examples of buildings, both grand and modest which have been decorated with this most appealing of colour combinations to enrich and brighten the lives of their occupants.

We gain our inspiration from the natural world that surrounds us, in which the range of blues is almost infinite, spanning the whole spectrum from the palest grey-blue to the most intense cerulean. In the natural world the combination of blue and white can be found whenever we look around us, wherever we are – in white-capped seas, white clouds floating in a blue sky, gleaming icicles, vibrant or softly hued blue flowers, shimmering butterflies, iridescent birds, so it is hardly surprising that these colours have always inspired us.

13

LEFT Sunlight filters through hundreds of small holes in the domed roof of this Turkish bath in Bursa, where it reflects on the surface of the turquoise water in the pool, throwing light into the recesses.

ABOVE Graded dark blue tiles follow the contour of these swimming pool steps. The main area of the pool is laid with turquoise tiles and the rim edged with a simple pattern.

RIGHT The interior of a mosque in the Turkish town of Konja. The walls have been tiled in a turquoise frieze, leading the eye up into the dome. The dome is tiled with a range of intricate motifs.

We have always decorated our homes, our domestic wares and our clothing, often as a way of recording the natural life we see around us. This instinct to embellish is the mark of a culture moving away from survival towards civilization, which is why the cultural heritage of the great civilizations is so rich. The skill of the craftsmen of Byzantium, Ancient Greece and Rome and the Renaissance is as much a marvel today as it was then.

In earliest times the primary source of colour came, quite simply, from the earth; tribes in Britain daubed their bodies with blue clay as a form of decoration. The clay was coloured with woad, a blue plant dye. Another source of blue was the anil plant which gave us indigo, a deep blue pigment used to colour cloth. Indigo is still an important pigment and it is used by everyone from local craftsmen in the developing world to the leading fashion houses of Europe.

The Middle East was the cradle that nurtured blue, and it was the discovery of the cobalt blue pigment, probably in Baluchistan, which introduced this wonderful intense blue into the decorative arts of both that region and the many parts of the world with which it traded. Byzantine and Islamic mosaics and Chinese porcelain would all have been poor shadows of their glorious hues had the craftsmen been without this colour; and it was the drive to emulate these beautiful and much-coveted wares which led to the development of the European porcelain industry.

Today it is hard to imagine a world where paint was a luxury and colour was very restricted, yet in the past artists who wished to use vibrant colours had to make their own paints, grinding pigments and blending them to achieve the required colour and texture. Craftsmen would wait anxious months for precious minerals perilously transported by camel train and by sea, then would risk their own lives by blending the toxic substances to create the colour they desired.

Given the danger associated with this colour, its social impact was tremendous. The jewel-like painted interiors of the great churches and palaces with their frescoes and magnificent paintings were a startling contrast to the simpler homes of the general populace, helping to confirm the power and glory of the ecclesiastical and aristocratic elite.

Then with the advent of timber houses it became necessary to protect the wood from the destructive elements. Initially this was done with tar or bitumen, but these materials were slowly replaced with oil-based paints, the forerunners of the modern paints we use today.

RIGHT The magnificent ballroom in the former British Embassy in Istanbul is dominated by two huge crystal chandeliers. Elegant white columns add a classical focus and divide the pale blue walls at regular intervals, with detailing around the mirrors and ceiling picked out in gilt.

16

LEFT The magnificent white pagodas of a Buddhist temple stand out against the dark blue of a Burmese sky. Some are ornately carved and others tapered. The points of each pagoda are adorned with intricate gilt helmets.

RIGHT This detail of the spire of a Turkish mosque in Konja shows extraordinary workmanship. The roof and walls have been covered with turquoise tiles, the contours of the scalloped design adding texture to its beautiful shape.

OPPOSITE A Chinese-style pavilion stands in a Swedish park. Its simple wooden door is made infinitely more elegant by the positioning of two columns on either side of it. A scallop motif outlined in dark blue has been painted above the door.

Islamic art is justifiably famed for the superlative quality of its mosaics, ceramics, enamelling and glass. Islamic ruling forbids all representational art and has concentrated instead on the development of a fantastic repertoire of intricate decorative patterns based on geometric forms and calligraphy. The use of precious or luxurious materials is also condemned and it is these prohibitions which, far from stultifying creativity, have brought about the magnificent flowering of Islamic art which can be seen in its great buildings, its gardens, its pottery and its carpets.

Glazed bricks, tiles and mosaics were routinely used to apply a decorative and durable finish to buildings. Blue, turquoise and green were the colours most frequently used. Each colour was fired separately to ensure that it was as intense as possible and the stunning results are still as brilliant today as when they were made. Mosaics were made in many elaborate shapes which would fit together to make panels of startling intricacy.

The finest examples of Islamic decorative art are to be found in their pottery. The establishment of trade routes to China meant that the two cultures inspired one another. Some of the earliest developments in Islamic pottery can be traced to fragments of imported Chinese pottery; and conversely tin glazed pottery with blue decoration by the Abassid potters is believed to have inspired the earliest Chinese blue and white porcelain.

ABOVE A classical bust on a marble pedestal graces an Irish ballroom.

ABOVE LEFT A detail of the painted overdoor in the dining room at Hylinge in Sweden shows two lions appropriately feasting on a bowl of fruit.

BELOW LEFT Two griffins form the focal point of this detail of a Swedish tiled stove. The tiles are painted with a neo-classical design.

RIGHT The edge of an exquisite Russian table which has been decorated with onyx, marble and other semi-precious stones and also ornamented with gilt. The top is made from lapis lazuli.

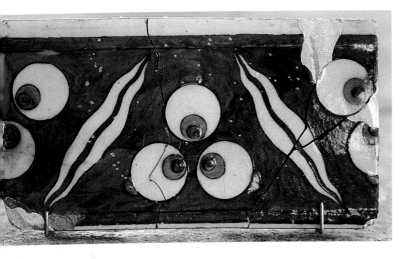

The Moorish invasion brought many elements of Islamic art into European culture, particularly the use of highly glazed tiles and mosaics. In Spain and Portugal the long tradition of manufacturing high-quality blue and white tiles continues to this day and they can be seen as decorative features on many fine buildings, from the restrained beauty of the Alhambra to the colourful exuberance of Gaudí. As the Moorish influence spread it could be traced throughout Europe in pottery and ceramics – the faience of France, Dutch Delft and Italian Maiolica all showed Moorish as well as Chinese influence. The calligraphic designs based on Arabic script became purely decorative devices with no understanding of what they had originally represented.

ABOVE Details from a selection of tiles:
An Iznik tile from Turkey with a beautiful and traditional design (above left). Fragments of Ottoman tiles (below left). Inlaid tiles from a building in Konja (above right).

RIGHT An Iznik tile panel from the wall of the Arab Hall which is the centrepiece of Leighton House in London. The Arab Hall was created as a setting for the tiles which Leighton had acquired on his travels in the East. It was designed by George Aitchison and based on the banquetting room at La Zisa, a Moorish palace in Palermo.

ABOVE A Federal-style, 18th-century clapboard exterior of a timber-framed church at the centre of a New England village.

LEFT An ornate balustrade of the 18th-century rococo Montagnes Russes pavilion on the Oranienbaum estate outside St Petersburg,

RIGHT A new look at Colonial style with this Walt Disney interpretation, adopted for a hotel at Disney World in Florida.

Covering the exterior of our houses with paint is a recent development. Its primary purpose is to protect the building, but the decorative element has always been a consideration. You need only look at houses in a Suffolk village, limewashed in colours from Wedgwood blue to ox-blood red, to realize that paint is more than a protective coating. When it comes to external decoration we should be guided by the colours around us – those that work best will be a reflection of the landscape. Hot intense colours look wonderful in India, but gaudy and inappropriate in northern Europe, whereas subtle colours are lost amongst the riotous palette of the sub-continent.

LEFT Rooftop sculpture by the Spanish architect, Antoni Gaudí, graced a selection of the houses he designed in Barcelona. Often of bizarre shape and randomly decorated with bits of tile, these sculptures also had a practical function, serving as chimneys and ventilation ducts.

RIGHT This detail illustrates the random mixing of broken pieces of tile and ceramic that was to become identified as Gaudí's trademark.

BELOW RIGHT Fragments of Portuguese and Chinese porcelain have been patiently fashioned into the shape of an ornamental duck.

In man-made as well as natural settings, the many shades and tones of blue blend easily and harmoniously. Modern skyscrapers clad in reflective glass become mirror images of the sky and clouds around them. The white surfaces of the Sydney Opera House are thrown into dramatic relief against the blue of the sky and the waters of Sydney Harbour. In seaside towns and villages around the world blue and white is the most frequently used colour combination, from the Greek islands, to Cape Cod or England's south coast; shades of blue stand in sharp contrast to pure white. Even in the most unnatural and built-up of surroundings it is difficult to associate ugliness with blue and rarely does a shade of blue, even at its most vibrant, strike a discordant note.

27

PREVIOUS PAGES Architecture around the world has used colour to outline entrances, exaggerate doorways and embellish walls. Nationally idiosyncratic, these examples illustrate the attractive wooden shutters of a stable block in Austria; an imposing doorway in Minorca, surrounded by inlaid fragments of tile; the use of dark blue paint, both matt and gloss finishes, to enhance a white wall in Mexico and even a simple outline in blue around a door frame.

LEFT The bright colours of purple and turquoise from opposite ends of the blue spectrum are embellished by the ornate wooden trellis and porch of this gingerbread house on the island of Mustique in the Caribbean.

RIGHT A restricted view of a narrow street through the window of a house in Goa. The clear panes, alternating with those of purple and turquoise, filter the harsh sunlight and throw interesting flashes of cooling colour around the interior of the room.

FAR RIGHT The exterior of a simple Welsh farmhouse gleams under a fresh coat of whitewash, the woodwork and cornerstones painted a contrasting bright blue.

As we look through the pages of this chapter with all the magnificent examples of the world of blue and white, and read the romantic stories of their making, it can be a dilemma to know how to apply what we have seen to our own lives. Few of us have a castle, a painted palace or even a picturesque ruin, and whilst we can admire, we also need help to know how we can use these ideas effectively in our own homes.

It can, in fact, be very simple indeed – it may be a particular blue which is just the shade we wish to use on a wall, for kitchen tiles or to paint a piece of furniture. Paint suppliers can now mix any colour paint you might want in gloss, satin or matt finishes and you should not hesitate to ask for their help. Take along the picture that has inspired you; very few people can accurately hold a colour in their head. With computer-controlled paint mixing, suppliers can now accurately match a colour from a swatch of fabric, a piece of china or a picture, but if you are having a colour custom-mixed, be sure to get enough to finish your job to avoid unsightly variations in a second batch of paint.

This book can also inspire you to be more bold in your use of colour. When planning a blue and white colour scheme, you may picture a fairly conventional blue and white palette, but on turning these pages it will quickly become apparent that blue encompasses a vast range of hues from deep purple to soft aqua and that mixing blues together is an exciting option.

A mosaic pattern can be the inspiration for a stencilled border. Traced off the page it can be photocopied, and if necessary enlarged, and then used to cut a simple stencil. A painted room in a palace can be scaled down and the elements of its design incorporated in a room of more modest proportions. A picture of a doorway with a broad band of colour painted around it reveals that this can create the illusion of a much larger entrance – a cheap and easy to achieve transformation.

Each picture should be viewed as a starting point from which you can develop your own ideas. To create your own world of blue and white you need to be inspired and it is far better to be inspired by the best than by the mediocre.

TWO

LIVING IN BLUE & WHITE

LEFT Imposing classical busts on gilded pedestals line a wall of this Irish ballroom, alternately interspersed with gilt-framed mirrors and intricately painted panels. The classical theme is continued with a line of busts on marble columns.

D ECORATING WITH BLUE AND WHITE HAS always been a magical formula. From earliest history to the present day, this combination of colours seems to have blended easily with the fashions and fancies of the period. What is the secret of its continuing success? First and foremost, it is a fail-safe formula: it is almost impossible to make mistakes as all shades of blue seem to complement one another. Secondly, despite being one of the most tried and tested combinations in the history of interior design, it retains a marvellous freshness. It never seems drab or passé, and always appeals. And finally, it remains, to my mind, one of the easiest and most restful decorative schemes to live with.

In this chapter we show examples of living rooms which illustrate the versatility of blue and white. A glance at the pictures will show just how varied any interpretation can be. From the grandest of rooms to the most simple these colours are guaranteed to combine harmoniously and give each room an inviting air of serenity and tranquillity.

33

LEFT A quiet corner off the master bedroom in this Majorcan farmhouse, designed by Mimmi O'Connell, uses bold blue and white stripes and patterned cotton rugs to create a cool contrast against the overall whiteness.

RIGHT Underfurnished simplicity in this small room near the Bosphorus. The louvred shutters filter the sunlight which reflects off the water outside, creating a soft, hazy interior.

It is sometimes stated that blue is a cold colour, to which I would say that blue can certainly be cool, but need never be cold. The geographical spectrum of blues is ample proof of this – from the sparkling white and palest ice-blue of snowy landscapes in the extreme north, to the intense blues of the Mediterranean, shades of blue deepen and become warmer as does the climate.

At its simplest blue and white living is to be seen in the houses of the Greek islands where roughcast walls are colourwashed in chalky blues or whites with woodwork and furniture painted in contrasting shades of blue or brilliant white; or in the bleached-out colours of the whitewashed cottages which border the coasts of northern Europe.

ABOVE The narrow entrance hall to architect Paula Navone's Milan flat. The industrial metal staircase leads up to the drawing room in this loft conversion. The blue tiled floor and washed, faded denim walls are linked at floor level with a neat row of blue and white tiles.

RIGHT Simplicity in these surroundings creates an attractive, tranquil atmosphere in this peaceful homestead. The plaster and wood have been whitewashed and the wooden table beneath the small window is covered with a simple white cloth. An old cotton quilt hangs over the balustrade.

LEFT There can never be too much of a good thing! Here designers, Private Lives, have confidently combined fabrics, ceramic vases and ornaments, books and even flowers to create an overall blue and white effect.

To my mind, our whole approach to colour has changed over the last decade or two and we are now open to a much stronger palette. With the advent of specialist paint ranges it is no longer simply a matter of choosing a paint colour, we also choose the finish we require – there are colourwashes, limewashes, scumble glazes and varnishes applied with stippling brushes, graining combs, sponges and the many other tools which were once solely the province of the specialist decorator, but are now familiar to most of us. Television programmes on home decoration were once only to be seen during the day, but are now mainstream evening entertainment with the experts becoming media stars. Stencilled borders and friezes are everyday decorative techniques which most of us have tried, and as we have become more experimental we have learnt how to balance the proportions of our rooms with pattern and colour. Manufacturers are producing ranges of historic colours using natural pigments to produce opaque shades of great depth and subtlety which look just as wonderful in a modern home as they do in a period setting, and despite their premium price we are prepared to pay the extra to achieve the effect we desire.

As we become more confident with colour, so we are more adventurous with pattern and will mix together checks, stripes and florals drawn from the incredible variety of fabrics on the market. Given the ease with which blues of every hue can be used alongside one another you can introduce a surprising number of patterns without it looking messy, especially if you use some plain blue or white fabric to pull it all together.

When it comes to blue and white decorative objects to use as finishing touches, we are spoilt for choice – whatever our taste or scale of investment – and you may well find it is more a case of knowing when to stop than how to start.

ABOVE A collection of blue and white ginger jars, vases, bowls and plates adorn a giltwood sidetable beneath one window of this classical dining room.

39

RIGHT These stunning vases are part of Axel Vervoordt's collection of 17th-century Ming porcelain from The Hatcher Collection, salvaged by Captain Hatcher from the South China Sea. Purchasers of these pieces included the British Museum, Berlin's Charlottenberg Palace and the Boston Museum of Fine Arts, but Axel Vervoordt's collection graces his dining room, where the table's mirrored surface reflects their beauty across the room.

LEFT, ABOVE AND RIGHT The dining room at the Castle of s-Gravenwezel, the home of interior decorator and antique dealer, Axel Vervoordt, is decorated in shades of white and palest blue reminiscent of the Swedish palette. The colours provide a setting for his magnificent collection of blue and white Ming porcelain. Although the glaze has degraded slightly after its long submergence, the romance of the shipwreck and the fact that the collection included designs never seen before meant that its value has remained high.

Of course the inspiration for your room need not come from a colour chart; the starting point may be a beautiful length of fabric, a painting or a collection of porcelain. A precious object can be the focal point from which the rest of the room develops. With blue and white decorating you can choose an almost monochromatic palette such as that used in the room featured on these pages, where a white colour scheme is the perfect foil for a prized collection of Chinese blue and white porcelain. It is interesting to picture how different the effect would have been had the owner chosen to set the collection against blue walls rather than white.

ABOVE The clean lines of this white biscuit medallion provide a striking contrast in colour and pattern to the blue and white toile fabric behind.

LEFT The dressing room to the bedroom which once belonged to Baroness Ottiliana Liljencrantz at Sturehof in Sweden. Simply furnished, as the neo-classical style dictated, the mouldings on the walls were painted by Lars Bolander, who was renowned for his mural decoration.

RIGHT This semi-circular Empire bench, with elaborate arm rests at either end designed in the shape of a lion's foot, is located in the Schinckel Pavilion in the park at Charlottenburg Castle, Berlin. The pavilion was designed by Karl-Friedrich Schinckel in 1824.

RIGHT The cool drawing room of a summer
house overlooking Bodrum harbour in
Turkey. Designed for comfort and
relaxation, the cool marble floor is
softened with huge scatter cushions and
long, low banquettes all in creamy white.

Unless you are a supremely confident decorator it is
helpful when planning a blue and white room to follow
the example of the professionals and prepare a colour
board. This involves gathering a selection of swatches
of fabric in your chosen colours and mounting them on
a piece of card painted with the colours to be used on the
walls and woodwork. Propped up and viewed from a
distance this will give you a preview of the effect you
will be creating and allow you to correct any potentially
time-wasting and costly mistakes. When you have
finalized your choice of colours and fabrics, make a note
of them on the colour board and keep this as a record for
future re-decorating.

Daylight and its effect on colour is an important
consideration when decorating a room. A white wall in
direct light can be dazzling, but will look quite grey in
shadow. Before painting a room you can check the effect
of direct and reflected light on the various surfaces by
painting lining paper with your chosen colour and
fastening it to the walls. This is particularly important
at the corners of the room where reflection can
dramatically alter colours. The type of paint you use will
also have an effect on the interplay of light and colour.
Matt paint absorbs light whilst silk, satin or gloss paint
will reflect light with the result that the same colour can
look very different, depending on the finish used. Matt
paint is better at disguising irregularities on wall
surfaces because of its non-reflective properties, whilst
satin or gloss paint will add life to dark rooms.

Artificial light is, by its very nature, much more
controllable than natural light, but it too will have an
effect on the colours in your room. Halogen bulbs are
recommended for pure, natural light. You may find this
rather cold-looking when used with pale colours
in which case tinted incandescent bulbs will give a
warmer light.

LEFT This elegant double staircase was designed by David Hicks for a neo-Palladian villa in Portugal. The flat wood balusters stand out against the air-force blue of the walls and the smart grey stair carpet.

ABOVE A painting by Elsworth Kelly and sculpture of two chairs by Dakota Jackson occupy pride of place in a modern loft conversion in New York.

Using deep shades on the walls of your living room is a very positive statement which initially requires some courage, but can be much more interesting to look at and live in than 'safer' pale shades. If you feel apprehensive you can experiment on a small scale with a hallway or a corridor which adjoins a larger room. Once you have gained confidence you will find that dark walls are a marvellous backdrop for any collection of paintings or porcelain which is thrown into sharp relief, especially when the wall colour echoes or pleasingly contrasts with a colour used in the decorative objects. I love to decorate in this positive way as I feel that it conveys my approach to life and helps me create a home which is both relaxing and stimulating.

ABOVE The look of a room can be changed instantly by putting chairs into loose covers. This corner of a country sitting room is dominated by the scent of a mass of garden roses on a carved three-legged African table.

RIGHT This large sitting room designed by John Stefanidis has comfortable chairs and sofas which in summer are covered in blue and white ticking, fresh-looking stripes and ikats. The room is always full of flowers from the garden, bowls of roses and plants from the greenhouse.

Decorating in blue and white can be anything from a complete all-over effect with walls, curtains, upholstery and accessories all conforming to the same theme, to an almost monochrome approach with just touches of blue or, turning that idea on its head, shades of blue-on-blue highlighted with accents of white. Although these are undoubtedly the dominant colours for the blue and white room, you should not be afraid of introducing other colours. It's amazing how a splash of contrasting colour can add drama; imagine just one orange silk cushion in an otherwise Mediterranean blue and white room, or a single shocking pink rose amongst a collection of blue and white china. The colour theme is emphasized by deliberate deviation and becomes more exciting.

LEFT The stairs, entrance hall and even the window sill and surround of this 18th-century villa in Cascais are lined with blue and white Portuguese tiles. The walls of the staircase are asymmetrical – one is tiled with a complete image, while the opposite wall carries a frieze to window height.

RIGHT A simpler, less sophisticated pattern of tiles has been used to line this doorway which leads into the hall of a Portuguese country house.

Like the other colours of the spectrum, the colour blue has many associations with the natural and artistic worlds. Yet we also respond to blue in a personal sense, and it is for this reason that we often have an emotional reaction, however subtle, to the use of blue in decoration and design. We feel colours as well as see them. A visit to Provence may well inspire me to decorate a sunny room in the hazy summer colours of that place with the cerulean blue of the sky, the deep purply-blue of lavender and grey-green of the foliage. My enjoyment of that room will not be restricted to an appreciation of a successful colour scheme, it will also recall the warmth of the Provençal sun and the scents and tastes of the south of France.

Mysteriously, you may find yourself moved to tears by the intense blue used by Chagall in his paintings, or the blue of a Madonna's robes and feel drawn to search for paintings or decorative objects which echo that colour; or repeatedly find yourself using a particular soft shade of blue which would not usually be to your taste, only to discover that it was the exact colour of a favourite childhood room.

Blue is a calm, sometimes even passive colour and has an air of tranquillity about it. It is a colour you can sink into and under its influence lose yourself in rêverie. Much used in Christian art it is the colour of faith, and to the Chinese with its long tradition of blue and white porcelain, the colour signifies immortality.

53

LEFT A drawing room in a villa on the island of Mustique in the Caribbean is furnished with a combination of bamboo-style and traditional sofas and loungers for comfort and coolness. The limed roof is raised to take advantage of the on-shore breeze.

RIGHT The late 18th-century salon at Bernshammar in Sweden has elaborate painted wall decorations by Pehr Emanuel Limnell. Between the windows are two mirrors with matching side tables by Pehr Ljung. The plain wooden floor has been stencilled to resemble more expensive parquet.

If you are starting from scratch with a room, choosing the colours to use can be a daunting process; it is often much easier if you have something around from which to make your selection whether it is a page torn from a magazine, a prized piece of blue and white china or a wonderful piece of fabric you have seen. Either way you will want to choose shades which enhance the feeling you wish to create in the room and for this reason it is helpful to remember that cool blues are those with yellow in them, in other words the turquoises and blue greens and aquamarines, whilst the warm blues have red in them and include the rich royal blues, purples and lavenders. Grey is a useful neutral colour which can be used alongside blue and white without diluting either colour. Like blue, grey comes in warm and cool tones and the choice of grey should be made from the same end of the spectrum as the blues you have chosen.

The sense of crisp freshness which a blue and white scheme conveys can be used to advantage in any type of living room – from an informal family room, or a book-lined study to the grandest of reception rooms. A sitting room furnished with comfortable sofas covered in flowered blue and white chintz, alongside antique pine furniture, with walls painted periwinkle blue and hung with striped curtains in toning shades would make a welcome gathering place for all the family and will withstand misuse surprisingly well, whilst a contemporary study painted in cool blues and furnished with simple clean-lined bookshelves and a stylish desk will create a calm haven for creative thought. A large formal drawing room has the scale and proportions eminently suited to the subtle palette of Scandinavian colours. These colours will heighten the elegance of their surroundings and age with grace and dignity, as befits a room of this style.

55

THREE

DINING IN BLUE & WHITE

LEFT The neo-classical dining room at Hylinge, Sweden, is decorated in blue and grey. The coupled Corinthian pilasters are painted onto the wall. The dining chairs are modern copies of a Hepplewhite design adapted from a Gustavian set also at Hylinge.

THE AREAS IN THE HOME WHERE FOOD IS prepared and eaten offer a myriad of settings for some of the most beautiful and natural effects in blue and white. Whether formal dining room, relaxed kitchen, sunny conservatory or shaded veranda there is an interpretation of blue and white which will enhance each room and appeal to you whether your taste is for clean simplicity or lavish opulence and because blue and white 'layers' so successfully it can be used freely on walls, furnishings and accessories.

THE BLUE & WHITE DINING ROOM

In the dining room a blue and white colour scheme has the advantage of looking fresh and light during the day and vibrantly rich and decorative at night. No other colour scheme can successfully achieve such a dramatic change of mood and the many shades of blue and white offer an extraordinarily versatile range of colours from the palest of hues where white and blue are almost indistinguishable, to the startling contrasts of dazzling white and ultramarine.

LEFT AND RIGHT An elegant conservatory-dining room in the home of the interior designer Nina Campbell. The table is set for an informal lunch using blue and white china and glass which blend superbly with Nina's fabrics. Blue and purple 'witches' balls look wonderful in a wire basket hung from the ceiling.
A close-up of the table (left) shows the variety of blues which have been used – a dark blue underplate with a blue on white white dinner plate topped by a white on blue soup bowl, accompanied by three different colours of glass.

The pale light and landscape of Scandinavia are characterized by cool grey-blues and were the inspiration for the restrained and elegant decoration of the Gustavian palaces of Sweden; but you need live neither in a palace nor in Scandinavia to make use of this understated palette of colours. To achieve a similarly subtle quality of light in warmer, brighter latitudes the light may be filtered through muslin curtains or shutters. A collection of Royal Danish blue and white porcelain would look perfectly at home in a room decorated in these gentle hues.

In the classic English tradition, a gleaming mahogany table looks marvellous laid with blue and white china and topped with crisp white damask napkins. There is a long history of fine dinnerware in this colour combination including the Staffordshire potteries of Spode, Minton and Wedgwood, and should you be fortunate enough to own such a dinner service it will be displayed to perfection on such a table. Equally

there is great charm in a harlequin table setting of blue and white china from many different sources, and the overall effect is so entrancing that the individual pieces can be of quite modest provenance.

In hot climates, the intense electric blues and dazzling whites of the Mediterranean and Caribbean are as appropriate used indoors as outdoors. The shady interior of a dining room which uses these colours both looks and feels cooler and provides a welcome retreat from the sun; a place where diners are happy to linger long after the meal is over. Louvred shutters or rattan blinds at the windows will keep light levels low but still allow good air circulation. Traditional Spanish or Portuguese blue and white tiles fit well into these surroundings and a table setting of Provençal pottery with its robust textures and designs accompanied by brilliant blue hand-blown glasses, such as those from Biot in the south of France, will provide the finishing touches to a simple but sophisticated room.

TOP LEFT The alcoves in this kitchen are 'splashed' with blue and white in the style of the porcelain made by the Gemundener Keramik factory. The shelves are filled with pots from Morocco, Japan and Persia, mixed with 19th-century Staffordshire. A blue and white tablecloth, napkins, tumblers and candles complete the effect.

BELOW LEFT The kitchen has been given the same tile treatment throughout, the table laid on this occasion with a crisp checked tablecloth and Gemundener Keramik plates and bowls.

RIGHT A plain, scrubbed square table is laid for a simple lunch. The chairs are designed by John Stefanidis and the gouache above the sideboard is by Teddy Millington-Drake.

BELOW A blue glass vase filled with fresh flowers stands on the kitchen window sill.

There is something about the random display of blue and white plates and dishes, tureens and platters, earthenware and fine porcelain, that delights the eye and warms the heart, and I consider no blue and white dining room complete without some of these decorative pieces, grouped together on a side table, arranged on an antique dresser or even wall-mounted.

At night, add drama to your blue and white dining room by spreading a sumptuous blue velvet cloth on the table and set it with an array of blue candles in silver candlesticks, sparkling water in blue glass bottles, an arrangement of flowers in a blue and gold toleware container and vibrant blue glassware. By standing the flower arrangement on a mirror you can multiply the impact of the blooms and reflect the sparkle of the candlelight around the table. All these details and more can easily be added to create a richly opulent effect for your dinner party.

ABOVE AND RIGHT My kitchen is a 'furnished', rather than a 'fitted' kitchen and is an immensely practical room, but also wonderfully decorative as it houses my lifetime's collection of blue and white china, glass and paintings. A floor-to-ceiling china cupboard houses the blue and white items in daily use and the pine half-dresser displays my collection of china. The blue central unit, which I designed and had built by Simon Saunders, houses my kitchen utensils.

LEFT Kate Dyson's collection of blue and white china is stored in similar style on a half-dresser.

LEFT Blue floor tiles characterize architect Paula Navone's home. The kitchen is no exception, where she has used turquoise glazed tiles as a splashback behind an almost industrial stainless steel oven.

RIGHT An aga is a fashion prerequisite for all country houses now and it is available in several colours, including blue.

BELOW RIGHT No detail has been overlooked here as even the pitcher, saucepans and curtain match the colour scheme.

THE BLUE & WHITE KITCHEN

The use of blue and white in the kitchen has a long tradition. Most countries have traditional designs of tiles and pottery which use these colours and they remain enduringly popular because of the calm, fresh quality they bring. I was moving house as I was working on this book and had planned a scheme for my new kitchen that was not remotely connected to blue and white, but as we prepared these pages and took the photographs to illustrate them, I was lured away from my original ideas as I reached the conclusion that blue and white was the freshest and prettiest combination and that nothing I could think of would surpass it. All my other schemes were put aside and once I had found one or two pieces of furniture painted in that marvellous French slate-blue, the rest simply followed on. By combining painted furniture with other pieces in plain oak an 'unfitted' look was achieved, and I completed the effect with striped fabric blinds and masses of blue and white china.

Blue and white for the kitchen need not be expensive. A dresser laden with blue and white china doesn't have to be filled with priceless treasures to delight the eye. Odd plates and cups look enchanting displayed together and a chipped jug can take on a new lease of life filled with garden flowers. Old French enamelware uses the blue and white theme on everything from jugs and basins to salt tins and soup ladles. It looks charming in the kitchen and can still be collected inexpensively.

LEFT Blue was the obvious colour for this kitchen belonging to a prominent member of the Conservative party. Designed by John Lewis of Hungerford the maple wood table, chairs and Corian work surfaces introduce a welcome relief from the solid use of one colour.

RIGHT The splashbacks around the walls are made up of predominantly white tiles, interspersed at regular intervals with blue ones, on which a further pattern of paler blue has been applied.

Blue and white is so wonderfully versatile that it lends itself to every sort of kitchen. You can opt for all-modern or all-traditional or create an innovative combination of the two using, for instance, a beautiful old blue and white nineteenth-century bowl as a centrepiece alongside contemporary, dishwasher-friendly china, glass and cutlery. Clean-cut, all-white units create a monochrome setting for bold blue china and cookware, whilst a pretty blue and white tablecloth transforms the kitchen table into something smarter for evening suppers.

Essentials, too, can play on the blue and white theme with tea-towels, waste bins, washing-up bowls, utensils and tins all easily and cheaply available.

RIGHT A close-up of my kitchen table laid for lunch with my favourite handblown blue glass napkin rings by Anthony Stern of Battersea.

In a traditional kitchen the windows can be hung with crisp blue and white curtains in checked gingham or striped 'dish-cloth' fabric and with the addition of a cosy blue Aga stove you will have achieved the essence of every English country kitchen. You can almost smell the baking bread and touch the scrubbed surface of the old pine table.

The innate beauty of blue and white china, pottery and porcelain lends itself to display rather than concealment. Why hide these beautiful objects away in cupboards when they can make their own contribution to the decoration of the kitchen? A pretty plate rack above the sink is both practical and decorative, whilst open shelves and tiled alcoves allow you to view a selection of many of your favourite blue and white treasures. A traditional dresser is still one of the prettiest ways of displaying china and, even if space is a problem, a shallow dresser can be placed against a wall which does not have sufficient depth for conventional kitchen units. Blue and white comes in so many different shades, all of which can, and do, mix successfully together, so limiting yourself to a particular style, colour or design is purely a matter of personal preference. Deep blue glass looks wonderful displayed amongst blue and white china as it intensifies the blue in the patterns, whilst clear glass seems to take on an extra sparkle in this setting.

ALFRESCO BLUE & WHITE DINING

No matter what the climate, all of us enjoy eating alfresco at some time during the year, and once again the blue and white theme is perfect for outdoor living. A wicker picnic hamper filled with rustic blue and white china, unpacked onto a handwoven cloth spread with delicious summer fruits, salads and crusty bread will look temptingly inviting.

ABOVE Undecorated white porcelain figurines are a pleasing contrast to the many different shades of blue in this pretty table setting.

RIGHT A dining room by Genevieve Weaver uses blue and white china and glass to create colour accents on the walls, on top of the elaborate gilt console table and in the table settings. The warm tones of this room reflect in the superb Venetian glass mirror to create the perfect ambience for evening entertaining.

ABOVE LEFT A table set with blue and white china and clear glasses is perfect for open-air dining in the welcoming shade of a covered terrace in a garden on the island of Mustique.

ABOVE RIGHT Irises and cow parsley replace the sunflowers, a blue and white tablecloth designed by Lillian Williams is draped over the rustic table and the scene is set for a more formal lunch on this cool terrace.

RIGHT Scattered cushions provide all the comfort neeeded for an impromptu breakfast in the shadow of an old fig tree. This garden in Majorca was originally designed by Cecil Beaton.

LEFT Gigantic 'sprinkle-effect' plates from the Gemundener Keramik factory in Austria, dark blue glasses and paler blue linen napkins, cutlery with dark blue handles and a riot of sunflowers from the neighbouring field augur well for an alfresco lunch.

71

Under a shady tree in the garden a table covered with a blue cloth is a cool haven from the summer sun. Use a blue tablecloth even when the table is not in direct sunlight as it is more restful on the eye in bright light than white. A jug of white daisies is a charmingly informal decoration which will go equally well with plain white china or a blue and white pattern. A summer picnic looks particularly inviting when spread on a checked blue and white cloth.

Even in the most agreeable climate, it is not always possible to eat outdoors and here verandas and loggias come into their own, providing many of the benefits of outdoor eating without the discomforts. With table and chairs permanently in place the table can be spread at a moment's notice with a cotton cloth and blue and white china, to offer a perfect setting for breakfast in the gentle morning sunshine, an informal lunch with friends, or a romantic candlelit dinner. A posy of fresh flowers from the garden will complete the picture.

LEFT Simple metal shelving has been created in two alcoves in this Italian kitchen. Lined with highly glazed turquoise tiles, the alcoves house a motley collection of jugs and glassware. The white-washed wall is decorated with an unusual tile design where it meets the tiled floor.

ABOVE A collection of creamware is stored on a shelf along a wall lined with an assortment of modern blue and white tiles.

RIGHT A four-drawer cutlery box, silver table ornaments, glass and porcelain are stored away in this neatly kept pantry.

ABOVE AND LEFT A detail of the half-dresser in my kitchen, showing a favourite set of French chocolate pots and some of my collection of 19th-century Bristol Blue glass.
The swans are amongst my favourite blue and white pieces. I believe that they were made in Portugal in the 19th century from fragments of 17th- and 18th-century Chinese ceramics.

RIGHT A single white shelf cuts across the uniformity of a wall of assorted blue and white tiles. where items in daily use, such as a stack of glasses and a coffee set of local pottery, are kept for easy access.

THE CONSERVATORY DINING ROOM

Conservatories are popular once more, although these days few of them are devoted simply to plants; instead it is a room which has all the light and airiness of the outdoors, but thanks to modern technology, remains warm and comfortable even in mid-winter. A conservatory makes a wonderful dining room and decorated in blue and white it will always look fresh and welcoming. Some colours look fussy and drab against a backdrop of greenery, but blue and white retains its charm. Metalwork benches and chairs painted in the traditional Georgian blue-grey look marvellous in a conservatory when piled high with plump cushions upholstered in blue and white ticking, bold stripes and checks. Fabric or rattan blinds hung at the windows and in the roof are essential for shade or to shut out bad weather. For a summer lunch a table setting of blue and white china looks stunning with vases of bright blue cornflowers, whilst the spring table decorated with miniature pots of grape hyacinths and lily of the valley is a perfect synthesis of food and flowers.

At night a conservatory makes the most romantic of dining rooms. Lit by candlelight, a table setting of delicate blue and white china, rich blue glass and antique silver will sparkle and reflect in the glass which surrounds it, and when further embellished with arrangements of fragrant white lilies and roses will provide the perfect setting for the perfect meal.

FOUR

SLEEPING IN BLUE & WHITE

LEFT This imposing bedroom is dominated by a superb 19th-century Anglo-Indian four-poster bed. The walls are covered with Indian cotton dhurries. On the bed is finely cut French linen topped with a periwinkle-blue handmade quilt.

NOWHERE DOES THE COMBINATION OF BLUE and white seem more appropriate than in the bedroom. It is restful, tranquil, cool, calming, unfussy, decorative – the list of adjectives seems endless, and as the illustrations for this chapter show, although the palette is limited, the interpretations of it are not.

Once again I feel that the reasons lie with nature, with the ever-present combinations of sky and cloud, sea and sky, light and shade. Blue and white is a natural union, and a union with which we, quite naturally, feel comfortable and at peace.

The bedroom is a very personal room to decorate. It is not just a room to sleep in but also a private retreat from the world outside, somewhere to recharge batteries and take time off from the pressures of life. In my bedroom I dress, do my hair and make-up, and surround myself with personal, pretty things. It is a place where I feel free to indulge myself. In creating an atmosphere which is conducive to all these things it is hardly surprising that blue and white often features in some way or another.

77

ABOVE This small bedroom is located in one of the guest wings at Elgahammar, considered to be Sweden's finest Palladian house and designed by the architect Giacomo Quarenghi from St Petersburg. The deceptively simple iron-framed bed is clad in a thin-striped blue and white fabric, its spartan appearance softened by the contrasting bed hanging. The chairs and chest of drawers are Biedermeier.

LEFT The twin brass beds and matching wallpaper and furnishing fabric give this bedroom in the same house a more modern feel. The Biedermeier sofa at the end of the two beds provides the only historical footnote.

RIGHT Lengths of fine mosquito netting waft gently on an on-shore breeze through the windows of this airy bedroom on the island of Lamu, off the east coast of Africa.

In my blue and white bedroom I have used layers of blue and white check curtains and blinds with embroidered curtains, all of which can easily be re-hung seasonally to create a cool look for summer and a warmer winter atmosphere.

Fine bed linen is seen by some as a luxury and others, including myself, as an essential. Historically, traditional linen lost popularity during the years of post-war austerity when lack of household staff and reduced circumstances forced people to look for cheaper and easier alternatives. Experiments with synthetic fibres resulted in sheets that never creased but equally did not breathe – a very uncomfortable experience. However, from about 1970 onwards, there has been a gradual move away from man-made fibres back to natural cottons and linens and a great resurgence in the popularity of antique linen. This began in the Sixties and Seventies, largely thanks to the hippie movement which started the craze for buying old clothes, partly because they were fun and partly because they could be picked up for a song in places like Kensington Market. The fascination with old clothes progressed to include old linen, lace and textiles. Today, every house sale and clearance that reveals a cache of old linen draws in eager buyers, enthusiasts for the past who are aware that old linen represents wonderful value for money. To re-create the same quality and fine workmanship today would be prohibitively expensive.

Today, modern technology and the manufacture of easy-care cottons have brought good-quality bed linen within the reach of many people for whom monogrammed, handstitched pure Irish linen sheets are out of the question. (Though I have to admit that personally, as I have already said, I consider crisp, newly laundered linen sheets to rank high on my list of priorities.) America led the world in developing easy-care, reasonably priced, pure cotton bed linen and it is still the market leader. However, there is new competition from countries such as China and Indonesia where skilled embroiderers are now producing beautifully decorated bed linen in the same way that earlier generations produced export ware porcelain.

ABOVE The gold fern finials were actually taken from an old mirror – all that was needed was a little re-touching in matt gold paint. The natural form of the leaves works well with the soft fabric of the drapes, and adds a subtle grandeur, reflected in the gold motifs on the roman blind.

RIGHT These blue and white drapes define the shape of the bay window recess. The larger pattern in the foreground and the smaller check close to the balcony make the recess appear deeper, creating a wonderful contrast between the bold blues and soft light streaming into the bedroom.

ABOVE An antique French day bed, painted white, occupies one end of this small country study. The room has been canopied with inexpensive blue cotton, and the pictures and objects, chosen for their decorative effect, perpetuate the blue theme.

RIGHT This airy bedroom is dominated by an imposing four-poster bed built of local mahogany, the height of its posts accentuated by swathes of fine mosquito netting. The sculptural quality of the empty chair on the bare cedar floor is enhanced by its faded peeling blue paint.

ABOVE LEFT Capturing the theme of blue and white to perfection, two Chinese vases have been transformed into lamp bases and placed on toile-covered tables on either side of the bed.

BELOW LEFT A collection of blue and white china is displayed on a blue iron stand with glass shelves. The cream and blue chair softens the overall effect and complements the cream bed covering.

RIGHT This elegant bedroom shows an inspired mixing of a blue and white toile fabric for the walls and curtains, highlighted with paintings and prints of Chinese bowls and vases. The addition of real blue and white porcelain is a clever touch which helps create a perfect room.

In terms of decoration, the traditional French toile bedroom still epitomizes true blue and white for me. The scenes of pastoral idyll have a romantic beauty to them which is perfect for use in the bedroom. The same toile is used for the curtains, bedhead, valance and bed cover and is even battened onto the walls. It also appears in any upholstery such as a chaise longue, stool or armchair. It is used uninhibitedly throughout and the pattern runs uninterrupted from one side of the room to the other and from floor to ceiling (sometimes that is covered, too). Woodwork is usually painted matt off-white or grey. Many companies now produce matching toile fabric and wallpaper which makes this scheme far easier to re-create.

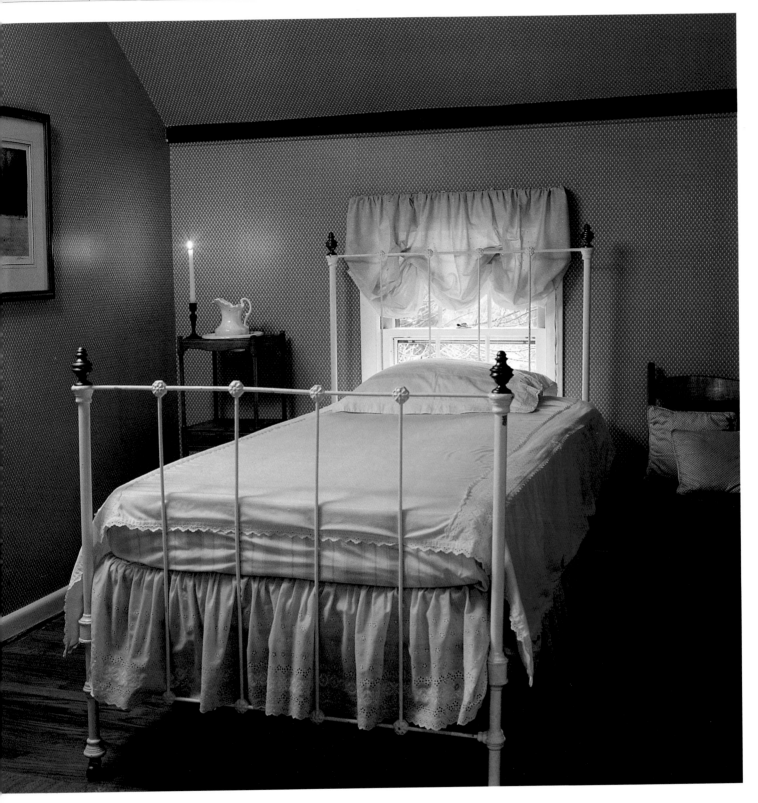

ABOVE One of the bedrooms at the Shaker village of Hancock in New Hampshire. The beds are narrow and without springs, a thick string used instead to support the sleeping frame. An unused chair is stored on pegs on a continuous wooden band around the room, along with other objects and a rail for hanging towels.

LEFT The small window of this attic bedroom is dwarfed by the white iron bedstead and there is a cheeky glimpse of blue and white striped undersheet between the lacy valance and matching cotton cover.

There are many other interpretations of the romantic bedroom. To some it may be soft blue walls, billowing sprigged muslin curtains and a traditional Victorian iron bed covered with *broderie anglais* linen. Others may prefer a contemporary look using bold patterns on walls and drapes softened by white lace on the bed. For a romantic look the light should be diffuse, filtered through fabric or shutters.

Muslins, calicos, cottons and pretty laces are ways in which highly decorative and very feminine effects can be created around windows and over beds. Accents of blue can be added in the trimmings and tie-backs, in the linen or simply in the arrangements of pictures, china and decorative objects.

RIGHT Two 18th-century French ceramic lions by Lunneville recline under the finely cut French bed linen and blue periwinkle Northumberland quilt.

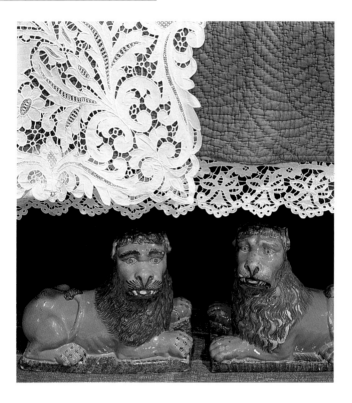

OPPOSITE A length of white cotton nailed across the window and caught with a thin band of braid and beads serves as a curtain, its ethereal quality exaggerated by the huge heavy tassels which hang as ornamentation on either side. The walls of this bedroom are lightly washed with blue and several checked rugs of different sizes and tones of blue cover the blue tiled floor.

How you choose to decorate your room will inevitably be influenced by where you live. Cool tiled floors, walls colourwashed chalky blue, and shuttered windows are perfect for a hot climate but can feel distinctly chilly somewhere cooler; whereas fabric-lined walls, quilted bed heads and thick carpets are appropriate for a cold climate but would seem stifling in the tropics. Although central heating and air-conditioning can now protect us from the extremes of climate and mean that we can introduce elements of a favourite style of decoration regardless of where we live, it is still not advisable to wholly defy our location – a room decorated in such a manner will be a conversation piece for a short while, but will soon pall.

Although a carpet is not always appropriate, a rug is always welcome next to the bed – even the Shakers, with their pared-down lifestyle, saw this as a necessity rather than a luxury. Rugs are wonderfully decorative objects which can look marvellous in a blue and white bedroom whether laid on a tiled floor, on polished wooden floorboards or on top of a soft wool carpet.

In other parts of the house it is usually necessary to bear in mind practical considerations, but in the bedroom I feel that these matters should be forgotten. If a cream carpet strewn with fragile, but beautiful rugs is your heart's desire then so be it; or if your mind strays towards a velvet-covered chaise longue piled high with cushions on which you may one day find the time to recline and read novels; this is your own private retreat and you should do exactly as you wish. Your bedroom should be a place which allows you to leave behind the usual concerns of daily life, a place of relaxation and quiet reflection which allows you to emerge refreshed and invigorated.

Central to the bedroom is the bed. We spend, on average, a third of our lives in bed, yet it is quite extraordinary just how many people sleep in an uncomfortable bed. Buy the best bed you can afford – a beautifully decorated bedroom filled with wonderful objects should be conducive to restful sleep and must include a comfortable bed or it will be of little consolation as you toss and turn.

ABOVE Twin beds festooned
with mosquito netting and
covered with a simple blue
and white cotton bedspread
make this guest room look
cool and inviting.

LEFT 18th-century panelling in
this French chateau has been
painted a classical 'gris tendre'.
The niche bed, draped
curiously in a Laura Ashley
fabric, has a secret door in its
back wall which opens onto the
bathroom.

In your lovely blue and white bedroom do make sure
that you haven't forgotten the mundane practicalities
that ease everyday life. A dressing table should be
positioned near a window so that you can apply your
make-up in good natural light, and should also be well-
illuminated at night, but this need not mean strong light
– low-wattage light bulbs tinted in warm shades are far
more flattering to the complexion and will do wonders
for your confidence. Sockets for appliances such as
hairdryers should be easily accessible and positioned
near the dressing table. Lovely old mirrors are perfect
for the bedroom, with their aged silvering they reflect
beautifully soft images which enhance both yourself and
your room.

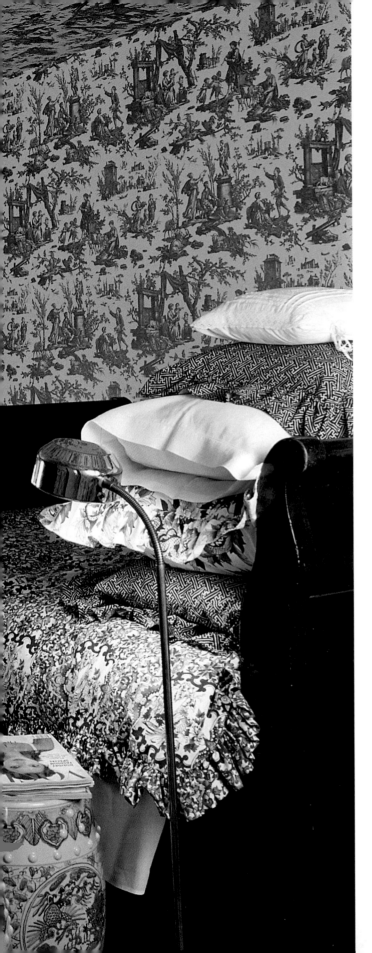

LEFT Designer Mimmi O'Connell describes her bedrooms as boxes and this one is nicknamed 'the teapot'. Cocooned in a blue and white toile de Jouy paper which covers both walls and ceiling, the bed is piled high with alternate blue and white pillows. Canvas blinds, rolled halfway, are tied with contrasting fabric that matches the striped dress curtains.

Because the bedroom is essentially a night-time room it is vital that careful thought is given to its lighting. A central overhead light is seldom necessary or advisable as it tends to shed harsh light and leaves you exposed to the glare of bare light bulbs as you lie in your bed. It is far better to have soft pools of light which illuminate only the immediate surroundings and lend the room an air of mystery and romance. Candles will give the softest light of all but most of us save them for very special occasions – daily use would be far too hazardous. Table lamps are ideal for either side of the bed or alternatively wall lights on articulated arms which can be set low on the wall behind. Off-white or cream pleated shades will glow with a soft light which is flatteringly diffuse whilst dark blue lampshades will throw dramatic arcs of light downwards, creating deep shadows around them.

If a more general light is essential, uplighters can be used to throw light up onto the ceiling and reflect it softly downwards, especially when they are fitted with dimmer switches which give you very flexible control of the lighting levels. Similarly, an old crystal chandelier, in all its decorative beauty, can look magnificent in a bedroom, but once again, it is essential that it is fitted with a dimmer switch or the light will be far too dazzling.

During the day, cream blinds can be used at the windows filter out the harsher rays of sunlight while still allowing a warm and diffuse light through.

93

PAGE 94 In this London bedroom designed by Anne Singer, toile walls, curtains and bedhead contrast pleasingly with the military precision of the pillows and the superb indigo bedspread.

PAGE 95 This blue and white bedroom in New York also uses blue and white toile on the walls, but as the backdrop for a pair of large Chinese watercolours and antique white bed linen the effect is quite different.

ABOVE A tiny bedroom on Juliette Mole's former houseboat which was moored on the Thames in Chelsea. The bed is scattered with cushions and doubles as a daybed and work space.

RIGHT The shelves of an Austrian cupboard are stacked with an assortment of fabric and linen, beautifully starched and ironed. Pomanders and muslin bags filled with lavender keep the cupboard smelling sweet.

Storage is an important element in any bedroom. It is essential to have ample wardrobe and drawer space to keep your clothes looking their best and to allow easy access. A pretty armoire is decorative but seldom spacious enough for your needs. In a toile de Jouy bedroom, hanging space would be concealed by covering cupboard doors with the same fabric as used on the walls. This type of 'hidden' storage is a good way of keeping a room looking uncluttered. Space permitting, of course, a walk-in wardrobe is the ideal solution, but it is also nice to display some of your more decorative possessions. A hat collection can look as good as a group of pictures on a wall and a glass-fronted cupboard reveals neatly folded linens.

FIVE

BATHING IN BLUE & WHITE

LEFT A bathroom in Piers von Westenholz's country house is lined with tongue-and-groove panelling and has been painted blue throughout. A double wash basin and a set of ivory-backed brushes add a touch of grandeur.

O F ALL THE ROOMS IN THE HOUSE IT SEEMS that blue and white is least often associated with the bathroom. Perhaps this is because it is not considered a warm and cosy combination; it may also be because traditional marbles are more often pink or green in tone, and colour schemes evolved from their colouring. Whatever the reasons, I consider blue and white a stunning combination and as suitable for the bathroom as any other room in the house Nowadays with good heating and plentiful hot water, cool colours can be used freely.

It is interesting to note that, historically, blue did feature in the original 'fitted' bathrooms. Made by companies such as Doultons and Twyfords, the early lavatories were decorated both inside and out with colourful designs. The bowls were printed or painted with a variety of fruit, flower or willow patterns before being glazed; blue was a popular colour along with red and pink. These elaborate pieces are now much sought-after antiques and can still be found, together with their original high-level cisterns with chain pulls.

99

With the increased popularity of the more traditional style of bathroom fittings there are antique dealers and reclamation yards which can supply everything from original taps and chrome towel rails to extraordinary nineteenth-century shower cubicles which look as if they could have inspired H G Wells's time machine! When renovating an old bathroom or planning a new one it is worthwhile taking the time to visit your local specialists to see what is available. Even if you cannot afford to buy all old fittings you can still give your bathroom a period look by combining one old piece, say a hand basin, or even just original taps or old tiles, with modern copies of the old bathroom fittings. Today many manufacturers are even making reproductions of the antique blue and white lavatories and basins which will certainly give an authentic touch to traditional-style bathrooms, particularly when paired with a roll-top cast-iron bath on claw feet. Before embarking on a bathroom which includes old fittings it is recommended that you find yourself a plumber who is not overwhelmed by the far-from-standard nature of much of the pipework which will be needed to make it function. Although bargains can still be found, a cheap price may indicate there is something wrong or missing. A good plumber will be happy to check over any proposed purchase and give you an idea of the time and expense involved in getting it into working order. This can help you avoid expensive mistakes.

LEFT The decorative theme for this bathroom in a Malibu beach house designed by Dot Spikings would appear to have been inspired by the large painting hanging above the bath. Linen blinds and a simple wicker chair complete the picture.

RIGHT A novel storage idea has been introduced in this bathroom, where two rows of beautifully ironed shirts hang from a rail designed like a form of scaffolding.

LEFT AND RIGHT A mixture of different tiles is used to theatrical effect in this Italian bathroom. The narrow entrance is visually enhanced with a tile border around the doorway. The walls are decorated with glazed tiles of irregular hues of blue and continuity throughout the apartment is maintained by the floor tiles. Spartan rather than comfortable, the only furniture in this bathroom is an iron chair and towel stand, both painted a pale verdigris.

After a rather unfortunate detour into coloured bathroom suites in the Sixties and Seventies most of us have returned to the safety of white bathroom fittings. I find that even the simplest all-white bathroom can be given a new lease of life just by adding a blue glass, china, towels and fabrics. For instance a contemporary bathroom can be given a very fresh summery look with accessories and towels in forget-me-not blue, billowing white muslin curtains, a glass vase of seasonal blue and white flowers and a painted cane chair with plump cushions upholstered in a pretty striped fabric.

Most modern bathrooms are very compact and a major improvement can be made by the provision of additional space, or even the illusion of space. If you are someone who always prefers a shower, and yet a large part of the bathroom is taken up with a bath, you should consider removing it and installing a luxurious tiled shower. There are wonderful handmade tiles in rich shades of blue which, when mixed together, have all the opulence of a traditional Turkish bath. If you are unwilling to sacrifice your bath you can still create a feeling of space by replacing one, or even better, two tiled walls with mirrors. The resulting reflections will create an enormously increased sense of space. Like tiles, mirrors can be drilled using a special drill bit which will allow you to mount lights on these walls and glass shelves for storage and display. Use soft lighting, however, or the effect will be too dazzling.

LEFT A wonderful collection of blue and white porcelain 'loo pulls' c. 1890 demonstrates how practically anything looks more decorative when shown 'en masse'.

RIGHT Patriotism has taken hold of this bathroom decorated in memory of Queen Victoria. The shagpile carpet has been designed to resemble the Union Jack and the walls are adorned with a mixed assortment of prints and memorabilia. A bronze bust of Queen Victoria stands on a stripped pine column.

LEFT A tranquil white bathroom in Axel Vervoordt's castle. A carved marble armchair dominates an otherwise simple bathroom and subtle touches of pale and dark blue contribute to the simple air of elegance of this room.

ABOVE RIGHT Hand-appliquéd cotton trim on cotton bath towels from the Monogrammed Linen Shop in London.

CENTRE RIGHT Hand-embroidered monograms and a scallop-shaped edging give towels a decorative finish.

BELOW RIGHT Go for a homemade effect by simply tying bundles of towels together.

In the same way kitchens now favour the 'unfitted' look, the 'unfitted' style is increasingly popular in bathrooms and is wonderfully suited to a blue and white theme. To work well you do need a reasonably large bathroom or you are in danger of sacrificing function on the altar of style. If you are converting an adjoining bedroom into an ensuite bathroom this is a style to consider as it has much more the appearance of a comfortable living space than does a more conventional bathroom.

For a bathroom with a country look, floorboards can be uncovered and scattered with cotton rugs, and tongue-and-groove boarding fastened to the walls and painted hyacinth blue. With an antique pine press to store towels, a comfortable chair and a roll-top bath on legs positioned centrally against one wall, the bathroom becomes a wonderful retreat to linger in and enjoy.

If a richer, warmer look is more to your taste, you could consider using an antique or reproduction blue and white lavatory and basin with dark polished mahogany fittings accompanied by a bath with a matching mahogany surround. With deep blue paintwork, a patterned wallpaper, lots of pictures on the wall, and a nice thick carpet you have all the ingredients for a traditional bathroom full of creature comforts. Further enhance the mood with draped curtains at the windows looped back to reveal shutters or blinds. These will combine to keep the light level low as will the use of shaded light fittings.

ABOVE LEFT Natural blues often evoke a Mediterranean feel – here, the colours appear barely dry, running along the clay ridges of hand-painted pots. Placed near a rough plaster wall, this makes for an intriguing mix of creams and whites.

CENTRE LEFT The painterly quality of this blue linework on porcelain has elegance and sophistication, and works well alongside the naive pattern of the pots. Although the styles appear opposite, the curves of both flower motifs are a vivid, sensuous combination.

BELOW LEFT An example of the wide variety of decorative finishes available in lavatories during the late 19th century.

RIGHT A wonderful group of antique blue and white lavatories dating from 1880–1905. During that time seventy-five per cent of all bathroom fittings were blue and white and came from such important manufacturers as Dresden and Spode.

LEFT A Victorian canopy shower-bath painted a brilliant powder blue is both highly decorative and very practical. The screen is no longer necessary to keep draughts at bay but can create areas of privacy within a modern bathroom.

One of my favourite luxuries in my bathroom is an ample supply of thick, fluffy, white towels warmed on a heated rail -- nothing is more inviting. In fact I consider good-quality towels a necessity not a luxury, but I do like to ring the changes for different effects: blue monograms on white towels or white monograms on blue towels, or sometimes a white bath sheet topped with a handtowel and face cloth in blue or vice versa. A good selection of blue and white towels in varying sizes will allow you to change the mood of your bathroom in an instant. Picture an all-white bathroom and how different it looks when plain blue towels are used instead of white. As all blues blend well and there is no fear of making a mistake, you can use three or four different blues on the same towel rail graded from dark to light, and your extra towels will look pretty piled on a shelf tied up with a checked blue and white ribbon.

One of the ways we judge a good hotel is by the quality of its bathroom and the accompanying towels, robes and toiletries. A windowless box with thin towels and cheap soap will not be memorable, but a light airy bathroom with a plentiful supply of lovely towels, luxurious bathrobes and fine-quality toiletries is an experienced to be savoured. Take note of the things you particularly enjoy and introduce them to your own bathroom. In particular, the best hotels seem to find bathrobes which are longer, thicker and more absorbent than usual. Treat yourself to one from the hotel (they are usually for sale) or buy one from a reputable maker. Buy the biggest robe you can find, as they will always shrink when laundered and a robe is far better too big than too small.

Fine soap and fragrant bath oils add immeasurably to the pleasures and satisfaction of the bath. Don't wait to be given them, buy them for yourself – it is after all, a modest indulgence.

ABOVE A wonderful array of towels, piled high on an antique wooden towel rail. The large oil painting of a grandmother and two children gives exactly the right feel to this small space. People are often frightened to use large paintings in small spaces, but doing so actually increases the feeling of space.

SIX

BLUE & WHITE
COLLECTIONS

LEFT Interior decorator Roger Banks-Pye of Colefax and Fowler was an enthusiastic collector of anything blue and white. From Chinese porcelain to enamel mugs, the shelves in his kitchen almost buckle under their combined weight.

I HAVE ALWAYS LOVED BLUE AND WHITE porcelain and I believe that more than anything else it epitomizes the extraordinary allure of these colours. Although these pages do show some serious collections of porcelain, built up over the years by expert collectors, the joy of blue and white is that it can cater for all tastes and pockets. You can put your name down with an antique dealer and gradually build up an entire dinner service or you can pick up pieces here and there and put together a wonderful harlequin set. You can enjoy priceless jardinières and pots which are valuable investments or you can salvage broken jugs or chipped bowls to use as flower pots and vases – worthless in commercial terms, but much loved and treasured objects in daily use.

All of us enjoy the 'hunt', wandering through street markets and fairs, browsing in antique shops and bazaars in the hope of finding a little bit of blue and white china which may or may not be valuable, but which will certainly enhance a room. Once your eye is attuned to blue and white you will find it everywhere.

113

If you are prepared to buy damaged or repaired blue and white china you will find pieces for next to nothing which would be worth a fortune undamaged. You can still enjoy the pleasure of ownership with none of the anxieties and responsibilities. A piece which, in perfect condition, would be locked away in a display cupboard, can be in daily use. Find alternative uses for chipped china – I use jugs as vases with the flowers artfully arranged to hide the chips. Sugar bowls make ideal plant bowls and big bowls can be planted up with bulbs, the earth covered with green moss. Vegetable dishes which have lost their lids also make good planters and odd saucers are perfect stands for pots and vases to protect the table underneath.

114

ABOVE In a small hallway of my home I have arranged a geometric display of my antique tea caddies under framed groups of off-white intaglio prints. The contrast between the two collections is visually very interesting.

RIGHT A traditional Chinese red lacquered display cabinet, with two small drawers beneath one of the shelves painted with charming flowers, holds a collection of Mimmi O'Connell's blue and white ginger jars and Chinese pots.

Above a traditional mahogany sidetable, laden with family silver, narrow shelves at one end of this formal dining room display a set of plates decorated with handpainted flowers.

RIGHT Forgoing the formality of a laid table, assorted Chinese plates are stacked in readiness for a buffet. Crisp white linen napkins are tied with a length of dark blue ribbon and cutlery is upended in a pretty Chinese bowl.

The history of blue and white china is a long and fascinating story, and like many other collectors, I was enormously excited by the discovery of the fabulous Chinese porcelain cargoes which have been rescued from the bottom of the sea over the last decade. The Nanking Cargo was the first to be salvaged, and the press and public alike were fascinated by this tale of shipwreck on the high seas, the lure of the East, and the amazing dedication and skill of salvage expert Captain Michael Hatcher and his team. Prior to the sale at Christie's in Amsterdam on 28 April 1986, record crowds queued patiently to view the sale, and people who had never previously ventured into an auction house joined the bidding in order to acquire for themselves a tiny piece of this remarkable history. There were bidders from around the world for the one hundred and sixty thousand pieces of blue and white porcelain which were auctioned over five days and the final tally far exceeded the original estimates.

PAGE 118 China perfectly positioned on a dresser is one of the most traditional but still most successful ways of displaying such objects.

PAGE 119 A display of blue and white china in front of a painting of the same subject. It may seem obsessive, but is very effective and gives the room real style.

LEFT One wall of Lebanese decorator Jo Thome's bedroom in Beirut is lined with pale blue shelves stretching from floor to ceiling. They house Thome's collection of blue and white china displayed with no apparent themes.

ABOVE AND RIGHT A Regency bookcase containing collections of vellum books, Bristol Blue glass, Chinese crackleware and powder blue glaze vases. This combination of books and objects is seen through the crystal drops of a 19th-century Venetian chandelier.

LEFT Ceramics of different periods and styles reflect changes in pattern and density of colour. The top plate is a modern design from Mexico, its dark colour contrasting with the paler, more intricate Chinese design of the earlier 19th-century meat plate. The bowl is an early Turkish ceramic.

RIGHT, CLOCKWISE FROM ABOVE LEFT An 18th-century Chinese teapot with asparagus handles from my collection; a group of large jardinières made of enamelled iron by Paris & Compagnie, France in 1860; a Ming design, Chieng Lung-period temple jar holding rolls of old parchment; a 19th-century splatterware jug on a garden table ready to be filled with white daisies.

Romance, mystery and adventure all play their part in the worldwide fascination and perennial attraction of blue and white porcelain. From the earliest examples which made the hazardous journey to Europe in the 14th and 15th centuries – rare and precious Ming vases which were available to only the wealthiest and most dedicated collectors – the love affair with blue and white has never waned.

The original outbreak of 'Chinamania' dates from the 17th century. It began, once again, in Amsterdam in 1604, when the cargo of a Portuguese trading ship was put up for auction. Captured en route from China, the cargo consisted of some hundred thousand 'porcelains' and its sale caused as much of a stir as did its Nanking successor almost four hundred years later. It stimulated so much demand that soon all the East India companies began trading in porcelain, most of which was blue and white.

In England Charles II made tea-drinking fashionable after he was given a small packet of it as a wedding present. Cups, saucers, teapots and caddies as well as pots, jars, urns, garden tubs, jardinières, fish bowls, moulds, jugs, mugs, dessert and dinner services were all made in abundance for the European market. Within 50 years Chinese porcelain had been transformed from a rare and precious collector's prize to readily available everyday tableware and decorative objects, painted with patterns which were specifically designed for European tastes. Blue and white was here to stay.

RIGHT A remarkable collection of Chieng Lung tea jars and canisters c. 1706–1797. The jars are exceptionally large and are very rare in these sizes. Originally they would all have had ceramic lids, but with the passage of time most of these have been broken and replaced with wooden or silver ones.

It was not long before European manufacturers, jealous of the success of Chinese export porcelain, looked to cash in on the market. State manufacturers in France, Italy and Germany tried their best to emulate the Chinese. The closest in appearance was the tin-glazed earthenware produced in, and now synonymous with, the Dutch town of Delft. The Bow factory in England, known as New Canton, was making blue and white porcelain from 1747 and its early chinoiserie-inspired designs are now exceptionally rare collectors' pieces.

By the 1770s, the English potters of north Staffordshire had perfected the art of transfer-printing in blue on earthenware, a much less expensive material than porcelain. Josiah Spode led the way, helped by fine craftsmen such as Thomas Minton. Domestic production gradually increased, helped by the fashion for tea-drinking and by a war-time duty levied on silver which fostered a demand for pottery teapots. By 1799, the tax on imported porcelain stood at 109 per cent, and more and more people turned to companies such as Caughley and Spode for both new dinner services and replacements and additions copied from the original Chinese designs. The ubiquitous Willow pattern created by Spode dates from the early years of the 19th century. Just as European blue and white developed directly from its oriental counterpart, so designs can be traced from East to West and back again in a fascinating international circle.

The first period of blue and white printed pottery in England was wholly Chinese influenced, with innovative artists and engravers such as Thomas Davis, Thomas Lucas, Thomas Minton and John Ainsworth all drawing their inspiration from fine Chinese ceramics already imported into Britain. As skills and techniques developed, a gradual 'Europeanization' took place and a practised eye can detect a Dutch-style 'Chinese' house or willow tree, or spot a Palladian arch on a Chinese pagoda.

Blue and white is a theme which has entranced ceramic artists the world over. The Middle East, probably Baluchistan, was the source of the cobalt used by the 14th-century Chinese potters and the range of this precious commodity can be seen in the vivid blues of tiles and pottery throughout the Islamic world, stretching across North Africa and on to Moorish Spain. The Topkapi Museum in Istanbul has one of the finest collections of Chinaware, brought back from China by camel trains for use by wealthy Turks and Persians who traded cargoes of cobalt in exchange.

From the blue and white tiles and tulipieres of Dutch Delft to the Willow and Wedgwood of England and on through time and place to the brilliant hues of modern Provençal pottery and Spanish faïence, the lure of collecting blue and white china is universal. It remains as fresh and appealing today as it ever was, and it is little wonder that those salvaged cargoes of precious porcelain remain so attractive.

ABOVE Detail from a blue and white enamelled iron Paris Jardinière from Guinievere Antiques, London.

RIGHT An extremely rare collection of 'half-jugs'. These were used as traveller's samples in the 19th century.

A good collection of blue and white tiles can be a fascinating document of the history and development of blue and white porcelain as well as a decorative delight. Intensely glazed Chinese tiles, the beautiful geometric patterns on Middle Eastern tiles, the soft hues of the Dutch Delft ware and the Moorish design of Spanish and Portuguese tiles are incredibly diverse in colour and origin, yet blend harmoniously into a glorious and complete picture.

ABOVE Examples of modern tiles available from the Delft factory in Holland. Keeping to the original 17th-century themes, each tile depicts a figure, an animal or an object.

RIGHT A mosaic of antique tiles, some Delft, from The Water Monopoly, London.

128

LEFT A row of burnished copper saucepans and their lids hang from hooks against a wall lined with assorted blue and white tiles in one corner of this Majorcan kitchen. Two local pottery bowls on a rough stone work surface are used for storing wooden spoons and utensils – their venerability is evident from the number of staples with which they are held together.

RIGHT Two details of the tiled floor of a Burmese temple in the Saigan Hills near Mandalay show contrasting themes along the same basic design.

Of course porcelain is only one area of blue and white collecting – there is much, much more to explore. On my list of 'collectables' in blue and white are blue glass candlesticks, vases and scent bottles; any objects in blue stone or marble such as lapis lazuli or similar (the exact material does not matter, it is the colour that counts). Also blue glass and clear glass 'drops' from old chandeliers which look so pretty when mixed together in a bowl or plate; tall, thin celery vases filled with blue glass beads; and blue 'witches' balls and decorative porcelain objects including tea caddies, ginger jars and teapots. I collect pure white china in the form of figurines, candlesticks and plates – they look wonderful on a shelf or tabletop or accompanying a table setting of blue and white.

There is a jewel-like quality to blue glass which makes it irresistible to the blue and white collector. Artistic glass-making had its beginnings in 13th century Venice since which time the best glass makers have produced wonderful examples of their craft in a range of blues, from a stunning deep blue to a wonderful opalescent turquoise. The Venetians guarded their secrets closely for nearly 300 years and it was not until this secrecy was relaxed that the techniques and skills could spread to other countries in Europe. Inspired by the Venetians, the Germans and Bohemians soon developed a fine glass industry of their own. The Bohemians, although best known for their ruby red glass, were also producing a rich transparent blue glass which was achieved by adding cobalt to the formula. The 18th century saw the arrival of fine glass-making in England and the wine glasses of the time are unsurpassed in quality – particularly prized are glasses with colour twist stems. Amongst the makers of coloured glass the most famous were based in Bristol, who produced a deep blue glass of wonderful quality known as Bristol Blue. This is much sought after by collectors – a collection of Bristol Blue is quite breathtakingly beautiful; it is a great favourite of mine and I have a number of pieces. Although old pieces are increasingly rare and expensive, Bristol Blue is still being made so it is not too late to start a collection of this lovely glass.

131

Today there are many contemporary craftsmen and women who are making beautiful decorative objects in blue and white, and this is a source of 'collectables' which should not be ignored. It is all too easy to neglect the modern in favour of the old, but modern craftsmen rely on their patrons just as much as did their predecessors, so, if we wish to keep these skills alive we must support them. If you find someone whose work you admire, such as a potter, ceramicist, sculptor or glass-maker, consider commissioning them to make something for you. Most artists enjoy working this way – making an item for a specific individual and a certain location – and you will find that there is a particular pleasure in owning something which has been made just for you. Put your name on the mailing list of your local contemporary galleries which show high-quality crafts and you will be invited to previews where you will have a chance to buy and also talk to the artist. It could be the beginning of a fruitful relationship.

Even if your interest is mainly for the old you will find that modern china, glass and accessories can look marvellous interspersed among a collection of antiques.

LEFT A pair of Bristol Blue jugs stand on the granite work surface in a corner of my kitchen. The large one, a present from my son Michael, is the biggest we have ever seen.

How you choose to display your blue and white collectables is just as important as the collection itself – the finest porcelain will be overlooked if it is dusty and ill-lit, whilst an inexpensive but pretty collection of blue and white can look deceptively important when arranged with flair.

I love mixing many different patterns of blue and white together as I find this makes for a charming informality, but I equally appreciate the dramatic effect that can be achieved by displaying just one important piece in a room, especially when it is carefully lit. Lighting is all important – an alcove lit by subtle, diffuse light will display collectables far better than the dark interior of a glass-fronted cupboard.

A small collection of decorative objects looks larger if it is arranged on shelves with a mirror backing, and in a small room this will also give the illusion of more space. A dresser is one of the prettiest ways to display china, but where space is limited use a wall-hung plate rack; there are some wonderful old country pieces in fruitwood or you could have one custom made to fit the available space exactly.

One of the most effective ways to display glass is on glass shelves in front of a window. The light coming through the window gives the glass so much more life and clarity than when displayed against a solid, unreflective background. Keep the shelf supports to a minimum and your glass collectables will appear as if suspended in mid-air.

BELOW Detail of the mother-of-pearl inlay on a chest of drawers at the Sursock Palace in Beirut. The ceramic handle is designed to resemble the iris of a human eye.

ABOVE, ABOVE RIGHT, BELOW RIGHT Dark blue glasses of various sizes are designed with matching glass plates in a harlequin pattern, some clear versions are elaborately engraved, while others are elegantly shaped.

135

SEVEN

BLUE & WHITE FABRICS

LEFT A selection of tickings is a marvellous example of the simple beauty of blue and white fabrics. Originally used to cover mattresses, this crisp and hard-wearing fabric is now used for everything from curtains to upholstery.

BLUE AND WHITE FABRICS ARE IN A CLASS OF their own. No other colour combination has quite the same magical effect and whether it be stripes or checks, toiles or chintzes, linens or damasks, almost every pattern looks better in blue and white. Although the appeal of blue and white is, in some ways, quite mysterious and unquantifiable, it is, nevertheless, a commercially recognized fact. Publishers have discovered that a blue and white cover picture on an interior design magazine will always sell much more successfully than any other colour combination. Possibly this is because blue and white fabrics have never been out of fashion. They are multi-dimensional: they look fresh and crisp by day, and evocative and beautiful at night; they range from the most mundane of fabrics – coarse-textured ticking stripes, dishcloth cottons and gingham checks – to the most exotic of fine silks, damasks and embroideries. From the deepest midnight-blue velvets through to the flimsiest white muslins and laces, there is truly something here for everyone.

137

FAR LEFT The fabrics piled high on these shelves are all antique – batik, toile de Jouy, ticking, floral, checked, striped and plain – 19th-century versions of the blue and white theme which was as popular and evident then as it is today.

LEFT Linen embroidered with blue monograms. A simple way of copying this is to use a transfer alphabet as a pattern and then cross stitch one's own initials onto a plain linen pillow case or towel.

ABOVE Fresh and crisp, blue and white checks are perfect for table linen. There is a wide variety of patterns to choose from and you can use either a single or a variety of designs in your room.

Historically, blue and white fabrics have existed ever since woven cloth was first made. Weaving was a skill which developed alongside the domestication of animals and the cultivation of plants. Although the primary reason these early people made cloth was to provide warmth and protection from the elements, it was not long before dyes were being used for decoration. The earliest cloths were laid out on south-facing slopes to whiten in the sun, while indigo, a pigment extracted from the anil plant was one of the earliest dyes. The oldest surviving examples of textile printing date from the 5th and 6th centuries BC, but records from tombs and other historic monuments show that printed fabric was around, astonishingly, from as early as 2500BC.

139

ABOVE A bold design of a full-blown rose.

LEFT A collection of printed and woven fabrics, all with exuberant and abstract patterns. These can add a modern note to a traditional room.

RIGHT A collection of throws and a bag all made with Pierre Frey fabrics hang on Shaker-style hooks in the hallway of a seaside home. This illustrates how visually effective different blue and white fabrics can be when hung together.

Rather as the blue and white porcelain of the East inspired new techniques and new patterns in the West, so the brightly coloured printed cottons or calicoes of India had a dramatic influence on European fabrics. First introduced by the English East India Company and its Dutch counterpart in the early years of the 17th century, these cloths were immediately very popular with the public, but less so with the European textile industry. They requested the help of their governments who then moved to protect their own fabrics with restrictions on imports. Not until the middle of the 18th century were protective trade bans finally lifted, but their repeal gave rise to one of the most famous of all blue and white fabrics. In 1760, Christophe

Philippe Oberkampf established his printing centre at Jouy-en-Josas. His fabrics were printed using copper plates which were larger than the traditional woodblocks and which could be more finely engraved. These first 'toiles de Jouy' were usually in blue and white or red and white and depicted pastoral scenes or neo-classical motifs. They rapidly became popular and were used for curtaining and to line walls, as well as for beds and upholstery.

In America, British trade restrictions prevented the mass manufacture of textiles in the colonies until the end of British rule. The earliest examples of European-style decorative weaving from America are blue and white quilted coverlets.

ABOVE A simple and attractive way of storing remnants of fabric is to roll them up and secure them with a length of blue ribbon.

ABOVE RIGHT These toile de Jouy fabrics remain household favourites. Their traditional Arcadian scenes provide a highly decorative touch.

LEFT An amusing and imaginative way of displaying these swatches of blue and white fabric. Their intricate patterns make them appropriate for covering small items.

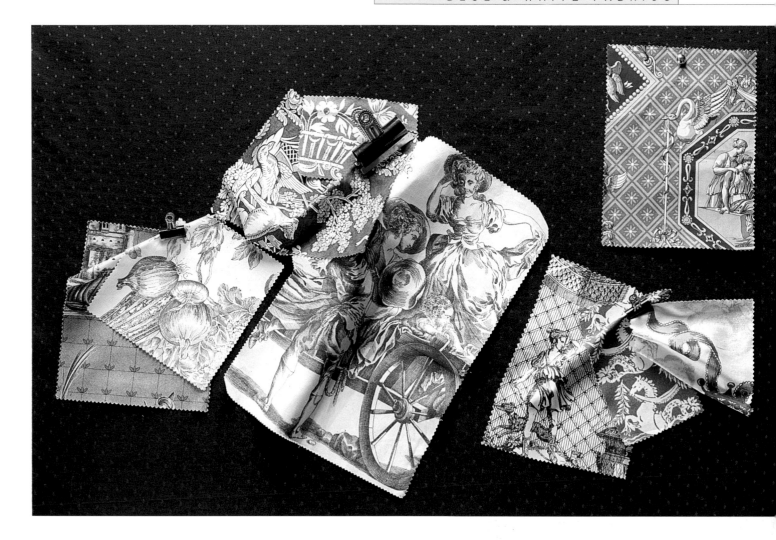

Today, we accept as normal the extraordinary range of fabrics which is available for us to choose from, but before the Industrial Revolution things were very different. All fabrics were handwoven and were accordingly cherished as some of the most precious belongings in any household.

The hangings that surrounded a bed were far more valuable than the bed itself. They were seen as the height of opulence which meant that embroidery and crewel work were seen as suitable aristocratic pastimes.

Blue and white fabrics have featured in one way or another through the centuries right down to the present day. Our own century saw the invention of denim or 'de Nimes', fabric first produced in the town of Nimes in France and without which our modern culture would look quite different. The selection of blue and white fabrics shown on these pages is only a minute fraction of the vast range of contemporary upholstery and curtain fabrics which are available. The range is breathtaking, from the toiles and damasks which pay tribute to the styles of the past and remain enduringly popular, to the freshest of modern checks and stripes. The very diversity of the fabrics shown grouped together helps to illustrate how well blue and white fabrics mesh together. As in the world of nature, all shades of blue seem to tone beautifully, and you will find that using this marvellous combination you can be wonderfully adventurous without the slightest degree of risk.

143

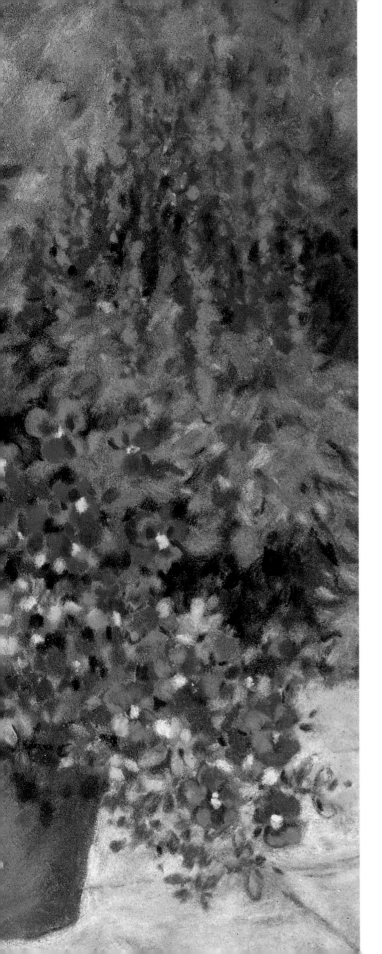

EIGHT

BLUE & WHITE PICTURES

LEFT A work in pastels by Maureen Jordan of a corner of her garden with the ultimate in blue flowers: hydrangeas, lobelia and pansies. Her paintings always sell out as soon as they come in to my gallery – a tribute to the appeal of my favourites.

I F THE WORLD IS DIVIDED INTO THOSE OF US WHO are passionate about a blue and white way of life and those who are not, then the choice of pictures for such a way of life subdivides us still further. There are, in principle, three very different approaches to selecting works of art.

The first approach is to emphasize the blue and white theme of a room by selecting pictures, paintings or prints which use only these colours both in the artwork and the frames which are also in shades of blue. By layering colours in this way, the room achieves an intense depth of colour which is dramatic but welcoming. When I worked with interior designer, Stephen Ryan for David Hicks, on a bedroom which used this intense approach to choosing pictures for a blue and white room, the watercolours I had commissioned, with their blue rope-twist frames, proved so successful and popular that it led us to produce a series of prints. These prints helped to enable blue and white aficionados all over the world to emulate Stephen Ryan's clean, crisp and dramatic style.

145

ABOVE A delightful painting of a tray set for tea by the Milanese sisters Maris Pia and Marinella Angelini. Paintings like this have always been popular, emitting as they do a feeling of hearth and home.

LEFT Paintings and prints of Chinese Export china are juxtaposed against real jugs and bowls to accent the colour and add depth to the room. What at first glance appears to be shelves laden with blue and white china is, in fact, a kitchen board – a clever trompe l'oeil illusion.

RIGHT A small watercolour of a teapot, cup and saucer set on a white linen doily in front of a blue and white tiled wall is the perfect painting for a kitchen, especially if it is hung between real china plates.

147

ABOVE This watercolour and gouache painting of pansies in a Nantucket basket by Meg McCarthy explores the variety and richness of the many shades of blue found in the natural world. A perfect foil for a blue and white planter.

LEFT Blue and white containers give gravity to the light, fluffy quality of the parrot tulips in this oil painting by Galley. The gaudiness of their petals makes a clever contrast with the cool blues.

ABOVE RIGHT Nahid Ghodsi's watercolour and gold leaf painting encapsulates both Persian style and western botanical style. The Persian blue gouache frame around the orchid makes it so effective in a blue and white room.

BELOW RIGHT The two watercolours balance the strong background, and make the flowers appear fresh and delicate. The handpainted music paper is a trademark of artist Christine Thouzeau's style.

The second approach to choosing pictures for a blue and white room is less obsessive but equally attractive and involves putting together an eclectic and multi-faceted collection of pictures which contain within them an item or items of blue and white: a blue and white bowl filled with flowers; a dash of indigo in a dress; blue flowers in a silver vase or in a landscape; a willow pattern cup and saucer. Your picture may only have a tiny detail in blue, yet within the collection that detail will become a dominant feature and will connect that picture with the rest in a marvellously disparate and unique way. This obviously takes much longer to achieve, but the excitement of the 'chase' as you hunt down each individual element is compounded by the effect of the whole collection as it grows.

The third, and possibly the most dramatic way to choose pictures for a blue and white room, is to ignore the colour scheme totally and fill the walls with a rich panoply of oil paintings of all shapes and sizes. I particularly recommend portraits in heavy gilded frames which create an effect which is at once dramatic and richly lustrous. Auction houses can be a good hunting ground for this type of picture, even on a limited budget. A fine portrait by a known artist will rightly command premium prices, but an unsigned picture of a long-forgotten merchant or provincial lady can often be picked up surprisingly cheaply.

Within and around these three differing approaches it can also be effective to intermingle blue and white plates, or other decorative objects, both old and new, amongst the pictures. This looks extremely attractive in any setting, but is a must when following the second approach. In general there should be some linking theme to the pictures; if not portraits, then choose a subject that appeals to you such as still lifes, wildlife, flowers or landscapes.

LEFT Collecting themed items in blue and white gives scope for a wonderful range of ephemera. Even the tiniest flash of blue on an antique tea caddy will sit well with a classic country milk jug, a fine willow pattern on a tea cup or an ornate tea pot of the deepest hue.

ABOVE Royal blues and golds complement an aqua-marine cameo, and vertical stripes of lemon create a soft, understated effect in this collection of Regency-style artefacts.

BELOW Preserves and their containers can be given the blue and white treatment. Motifs such as hearts, checks and flowers alternate in blue, white and yellow with trimmings of lace, cords and bows.

When deciding on which approach you are going to take when displaying a collection of pictures, it is important not to lose sight of the importance of the content of the pictures themselves. Although you want them to combine in a pleasing totality, each picture should have individual appeal. The pictures should look good next to one another but not be too homogenous – or you may as well use wallpaper. Even if the pictures have a common theme, their style and medium can vary enormously. Detailed watercolours, faded prints, contemporary and period oil paintings can be of related subjects, yet still retain an interesting individuality.

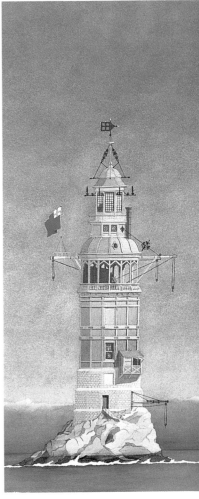

ABOVE In Andras Kaldor's watercolour of the first Eddystone lighthouse, off Plymouth, England, the feeling of shape, sea and sky make it perfect for a blue and white room.

LEFT A little blue and white goes a long way. This screen print of a Chinese chair and porcelain paintbrush holder has just small areas of blue — on the pot, and in a band of flatter pattern, parallel with the chair seat.

ABOVE RIGHT AND BELOW RIGHT Lise Le Coeur's oil paintings depict blue and white Delft tiles with trompe l'oeil. The tickets, envelope and key imposed upon the tiles evoke blue and white as a way of life.

How you choose to mount and frame your pictures will have an enormous effect on how a room looks. Single-colour mounts and simple frames will focus the attention on the pictures themselves and can give a room an understated look, whereas mounts embellished with marbled papers and decorative hand-drawn details, surrounded by highly decorative gilded frames, will create a richly opulent atmosphere. Changing the frames on a collection of pictures can dramatically transform them and it is worth taking time and trouble to get the balance right. However, you may find that sometimes oil paintings look best of all with no frame to distract the eye.

When it comes to hanging pictures remember that, unless you are a true professional, achieving straight lines and rigidly symmetrical blocks is fiddly and time-consuming work. There are few short cuts, and you will need to measure carefully and lay the pictures out on the floor beforehand. Standing on a chair or stepladder will help you assess the overall effect. A good way of checking if you've got it right is to take a Polaroid – this is a stylist's trick which will allow you to be more objective about the pattern you have created with the pictures. The balance of light and dark, and the overall shape of the display become more apparent – especially if you look at the photograph upside down! Making adjustments at this stage is much easier than when the pictures are on the wall. Once you are happy with your design and have hung the pictures, you can loosen or tighten the picture wire to alter the height of the picture without the bother of moving the pin. Do not be put off from removing the pins if you need to – pin holes hardly show and it is worth it to achieve the effect you want.

When visiting exhibitions and galleries take note of displays which have been expertly hung and look closely at the mounts and frames and hanging techniques.

If you are to make the most of a collection of pictures, good lighting is as important as the choice of frames and the careful arranging of your display. Whilst a picture light is appropriate for a single important painting, it does not work where a group of pictures are hung together; a single picture light is ineffective and using a light for each picture would be over-bright and messy looking. Spotlights on a ceiling-mounted track can be used to throw direct light on to the pictures, or if you prefer a gentler, more diffuse light, choose uplighters which throw light onto the ceiling from where it is reflected downwards. It is also worth investigating new, low-voltage lighting systems which are far more flexible and less intrusive than conventional lighting.

ABOVE LEFT AND BELOW LEFT
Galley, originally a ceramicist, meticulously researches her oil paintings of blue and white china. Her groups of tea pots, tea caddies or tea cups are bought with gusto by people wanting a strong blue and white painting. These works look especially striking when juxtaposed with actual pieces of china.

ABOVE Angelini's oil painting of three blue and white tea pots on a shelf revels in intricate and bold fruit and flowers, beautiful against their white spouts. This painting would be perfect hung in a kitchen, perhaps over a half dresser full of real china.

RIGHT Aloe in a blue and white pot, from a series by Mary Kuper. Created in watercolour and gouache, this painting is inspired by a series painted in the eighteenth century by Weinmann.

155

SUPPLIERS

LEFT This whimsical oil painting by Monica Schaars shows the wild and domestic cat, who carries potted preserves while her natural quarry leap tantalizingly close. The print dress contrasts with the raw blue-greys of the sky.

UNITED KINGDOM
Blue and white china, glass, linens, textiles and collectables can be picked up in antique shops, fairs and markets. The Antique Trade Calendar (Britain's Guide to Antique Fairs, Markets and Centres) is published quarterly by G.P. London (tel: 0181 446 3604).

GOOD PLACES TO BROWSE INCLUDE:

Alfie's Antiques Market,
13–25 Church Street, London NW8 8DT
Tel: 0171 723 6066

Antiquarius, 135 Kings Road, London SW3 4PW
Tel: 0171 351 5353

Bond Street Antiques Centre, 124 New Bond Street, London W1Y 9AE
Tel: 0171 493 1854

Camden Passage, 339 Upper Street, London N1 0PB

Chenil Galleries, 181–183 Kings Road, London SW3 5EB

Grays Antiques Market, 58 Davies Street, London W1Y 2LA
Tel: 0171 629 7034

The Kensington Church Street Antiques Centre, 58 Kensington Church Street, London W8 4DB
Tel: 0171 376 0425

Portobello Road, London W11

WEEKLY MARKETS INCLUDE:

Bermondsey Antiques Market, 158 Bermondsey Street, London SE1 3TQ
Tel: 0171 378 1000

Camden Lock and The Stables Market, Chalk Farm Road, London NW1 8AH
Tel: 0171 485 5511

Camden Passage Antiques Market, Covent Garden London WC2,

Charnock Richards Antiques, Fair and Market, Exhibition Centre, Park Hall Charnock Richard, Lancashire

Old Hornsea Pottery Antique and Collectors Fair, Lancashire Leisure Park, Wyresdale Road, Lancashire

Portobello Road Antiques Market, London W11

MAJOR FAIRS INCLUDE:

The Chelsea Brocante Antiques Fair, Chelsea Old Town Hall, Kings Road London SW3 5EE

The Decorative Antiques and Textiles Fair, The Marquee, Kings College, Chelsea, London SW3

The Fine Art and Antiques Fair, Olympia Exhibition Centre, London W14 8UX

The Grosvenor House Art & Antiques Fair, Grosvenor House, Park Lane, London W1Y 3TB

The International Ceramics Fair and Seminar, The Park Lane Hotel, Piccadilly, London W1Y 8BX

The Kensington Brocante Antiques Fair, Kensington Town Hall, Hornton Street London W8 7NX

ANTIQUE CHINA

Angela Heskett, Geoffrey Van Arcade, 107 Portobello Road, London W11

David Robinson *at* Magus Antiques, (oriental ceramics), 4 Church Street, London NW8 ATD
Tel: 0171 724 1278

The Dining Room Shop, 62 White Hart Lane, London, SW13 0PZ
Tel: 0181 878 1020

Gillian Neale Antiques, PO Box 247, Aylesbury, Buckinghamshire HP20 1JO

Jonathan Horne, 66c Kensington Church Street, London W8 4BY
Tel: 0171 221 5658

Nicholas Hilder (oriental ceramics), By appointment only,
Tel: 01608-659270

Peter Scott, 5–10 Barlett Street Antique Centre, Bath BA1 2QZ
Tel: 01225 466 689

Sue Norman, Stand L4, Antiquarius, 135 Kings Road, London SW3 4PW
Tel: 0171 351 5353

Ulla Stafford (English and oriental porcelain), 41 High Street, Eton, Berkshire SL4 6BD

CONTEMPORARY CHINA AND TABLEWARE

The Conran Shop, 81 Fulham Road, London SW3 6RD
Tel: 0171 589 7401

Divertimenti, 139 Fulham Road. London SW3 6SD
Tel: 0171 581 8065
and 45 Wigmore Street, London W1H 9LE
Tel: 0171 935 0639

General Trading Company, 144 Sloane Street, London SW1X 9BL
Tel: 0171 730 0411

Habitat
Tel: 0171 255 2545 for details

Ikea
Tel: 0181 451 2767 for details

Jerry's Home Store
Tel: 0171 225 2246 for details

John Lewis Partnership
Tel: 0171 629 7711 for details

ANTIQUE GLASS

Carol Ketley, 4–5 Pierrepoint Arcade, Camden Passage, London N1

Christine Bridge Antiques, 78 Castelnau, Barnes, London SW13 9EX

Guinevere Antiques, 578 Kings Road, London SW6 2DY
Tel: 0171 736 2917

Jackdawes Antiques, at Fulham Cross Antiques, 320 Munster Road, London SW6 6BH

CONTEMPORARY GLASS

General Trading Company – *see* Contemporary China and Tableware

The Glass House, 21 St Albans Place, London N1 0NX

Guinevere Antiques – *see* Antique Glass

Habitat – *see* Contemporary China and Tableware

Hands & Bannister, Camden Passage, London N1

Heal's, 196 Tottenham Court Road, London W1P 9LD
Tel: 0171 636 1666

Ikea – *see* Contemporary China and Tableware

Jerry's Home Store – *see* Contemporary China and Tableware

John Lewis Partnership – *see* Contemporary China and Tableware

William Yeoward, 336 Kings Road, London SW3 5UR
Tel: 0171 351 5454

ANTIQUE FABRICS

Belle Epoque Antiques, 40a Ledbury Road, London W11 2AB

Charville Gallery, 7 Charville Road, London W14

Hilary Batstone Antiques, 51 Kinnerton Street, London SW1X 8ED
Tel: 0171 259 6070

Marilyn Garrow Antique Textiles, 6 The Broadway, White Heart Lane, Barnes, London SW13 0NY *and* 498 Kings Road, London SW10 0LE
Tel: 0171 349 9110 for details

Patricia Gould, Alfie's Antique Market, 13–25 Church Street, London NW8 8DT
Tel: 0171 732 6066

Marcelline Herald By appointment only,
Tel: 0118 971 4683

Sarah Meysey-Thompson Antiques, 10 Church Street, Woodbridge IP12 1DH
Tel: 01394 382 144

Vivien Youlton, 277 Lillie Road, London SW6 7LL

CONTEMPORARY FABRICS

Andrew Martin, 200 Walton Street,
London SW3 2JL
Tel: 0171 581 9163

Colefax & Fowler, 110 Fulham Road,
London SW3 6RL
Tel: 0171 244 7427

Danielle, Flat 5, 1 Bramham Gardens,
London SW5 0JQ
Tel: 0171 341 9596

Decorative Fabrics Gallery, 278–280
Brompton Road, London SW3 2AS
Tel: 0171 589 4778

Designers Guild, 267–277 Kings
Road, London SW3 5EN
Tel: 0171 351 5775

H. A. Percheron, 6 Chelsea Harbour
Design Centre, London SW10 0XF
Tel: 0171 349 1590

Ian Mankin, 100 Regents Park Road,
London NW1 8UR
Tel: 0171 722 0997 *and*
271 Wandsworth Bridge Road,
London SW6 2TX
Tel: 0171 371 8825

Ian Sanderson, G13 Chelsea Harbour
Design Centre, London SW10 0XE
Tel: 0171 351 2481

Jane Churchill, 81 Pimlico Road
London SW1W 8PH
Tel: 0171 730 8564

John Stefanidis, 7 Friese Green House,
Chelsea Manor Street London
SW3 3TW
Tel: 0171 351 7511

Laura Ashley
Tel: 0171 736 6700 for details

Lee Jofa *at* Turnell & Gigon, Chelsea
Garden Market, Chelsea Harbour,
London SW10 0XE
Tel: 0171 351 5142

Macculloch & Wallis, 25 Dering
Street, London W1R 0BH
Tel: 0171 629 0311

Nobilis-Fontan, 211 The Chambers,
Chelsea Harbour, London SW10 0XF
Tel: 0171 351 7878

Pierre Frey, 253 Fulham Road,
London SW3 6HY
Tel: 0171 376 5599

Warner Fabrics plc, The Chelsea
Harbour Design Centre, Chelsea
Harbour, London SW10 0XE
Tel: 0171 376 7578

Zimmer & Rohde, 15 Chelsea Garden
Market, Chelsea Harbour,
London SW10 0XE
Tel: 0171 351 7115

ANTIQUE LINEN AND LACE

Diane Harby, Grays Antiques Market,
Davies Street, London W1Y 2LP
Tel: 0171 629 7034

Jane Sacchi
By appointment only,
Tel: 0171 589 5643

Lunn Antiques, 86 New Kings Road,
London SW36 4LU
Tel: 0171 736 4638

Spectus (contact Kati and Elisa),
Portobello Market, 298 Westbourne
Grove, London W11 2PS *and*
Stand V16 Antiquarius – *see* Good
Places to Browse

CONTEMPORARY LINEN

Caroline Charles, 56 Beauchamp Place,
London SW3 1NY
Tel: 0171 225 3197 *or* 0171 589 5850

The Conran Shop – *see* Contemporary
China and Tableware

Designers Guild– *see* Contemporary
Fabrics

Givans, 207 Kings Road, London
SW3 5ED
Tel: 0171 352 6352

Habitat – *see* Contemporary China
and Tableware

Harrods, 87 Brompton Road
Knightsbridge, London SW1X 7XL
Tel: 0171 730 1234

John Lewis Partnership – *see*
Contemporary China and Tableware

Lunn Antiques – *see* Antique Lace
and Linen

Monogrammed Linen Shop, 168 and
184 Walton Street, London SW3 2JL
Tel: 0171 589 4033 *and*
at Harvey Nichols, 67 Brompton Road,
London SW1X 7RG
Tel: 0171 225 2285 *or* 0171 235 5000

Ralph Lauren 143 New Bond Street,
London W1Y 9FD
Tel: 0171 491 4967 *and*
at Harvey Nichols, 67 Brompton Road,
London SW1X 7RG
Tel: 0171 235 5000 *and*
at Liberty, 220 Regent Street,
London W1R 6AH
Tel: 0171 734 1234 *and*
at Selfridges, 400 Oxford Street,
London W1H 1AB
Tel: 0171 629 1234

Universal Towel Company, Ashdown
House, 1 Spa Industrial Park,
Longfield Road, Tunbridge Wells,
Kent TN2 3EN
Tel: 01892 518 822

The White House, 40–41 Conduit
Street, London W1R 9FB
Tel: 0171 629 3521

White Mischief (mail order), Beorth
Park, Slugwash Lane, Wivelsfield
Green, West Sussex RH17 7RG
Tel: 01444 471 769

QUILTS

Anokhi Handworks, 105 Kings Road,
London SW3 4PA
Tel: 0171 376 3161

Chelsea Textiles, 7 Walton Street,
London SW3 2JD
Tel: 0171 584 1165

The Conran Shop – *see* Contemporary
China and Tableware

Damask, 3&4 Broxholme House,
New Kings Road, London SW6 4AS
Tel: 0171 731 3553

Habitat – *see* Contemporary China
and Tableware

The Indian Collection, 4 Castle Street,
Wallingford, Oxfordshire, OX10 8DL
Tel: 01491 833048 for stockists

The Java Cotton Comany, 3 Blenheim
Crescent, London W11 2EE
Tel: 0171 229 3212

John Lewis Partnership – *see*
Contemporary China and Tableware

Jen Jones (antique quilts), Pontbrendu,
Llanybydder, Dyfed, Wales

Judy Greenwood Antiques, 657
Fulham Road, London SW6 5PY
Tel: 0171 736 6037
Liberty, 220 Regent Street,
London W1R 6AH
Tel: 0171 734 1234

Ralph Lauren – *see* Contemporary
Linen

Valerie Wade, 108 Fulham Road,
London SW3 6HS
Tel: 0171 225 1414

The White House – *see* Contemporary
Linen

BATHROOM FITTINGS

C. P.Hart, Newnham Terrace,
Hercules Road, London SE1 7DR
Tel: 0171 902 1000

Colourwash, 65 Fulham High Street,
London SW6 3JJ
Tel: 0171 371 0911 *and*
125 Scrubbs Lane, London NW10
6QU
Tel: 0181 960 8983

Czech & Speake, 125 Fulham Road,
London SW3 6RT
Tel: 0171 225 3667

Max Pike's Bathroom Shop, 4
Eccleston Street, London SW1W 9LN
Tel: 0171 730 7216

Pipe Dreams, 70 Gloucester Road,
London SW7 4QT
Tel: 0171 225 3978

Sitting Pretty, 122 Dawes Road,
London SW6 7EG
Tel: 0171 381 0049

ANTIQUE BATHS AND WCs

Drummonds of Bramley, Birtley Farm,
Horsham Road, Bramley, Guildford,
Surrey GU5 0LA
Tel: 01483 898 766

London Architectural Salvage and
Supply Company (LASSCO), St
Michaels's Church
Mark Street, London EC2A 4ER
Tel: 0171 739 0448

Walcot Reclamation, 108 Walcot
Street, Bath BA1 5BG
Tel: 01225 444 404

The Water Monopoly, 16 Longdale
Road, London NW6 6RD
Tel: 0171 624 2636

TILES

Elon, 66 Fulham Road, London
SW3 6HH
Tel: 0171 460 4600

Fired Earth, 102 Portland Road,
London W11 4LX
Tel:0171 221 4825 *and*
117–119 Fulham Road, London
SW3 6RL
Tel: 0171 589 0489

Jonathan Horne – *see* Antique China

Paris Ceramics, 583 Kings Road,
London SW3 2EH
Tel: 0171 371 7778

Rye Tiles, 12 Connaught Street,
London W2 2AF
Tel: 0171 723 7278

World's End Tiles, British Rail Yard,
Silverthorne Road, London SW8 3HE
Tel: 0171 819 2100

DECORATIVE ACCESSORIES

Asprey, 165 New Bond Street,
London W1 0AR
Tel: 0171 493 6767

Colefax and Fowler, – *see*
Contemporary Fabrics

General Trading Company – *see*
Contemporary China and Tableware

Genevieve Lethu, 132 Brompton Road
London SW3 1HV

Graham & Green, 10 Elgin Crescent
London W11 2J8
Tel: 0171 727 4594 *and*
164 Regents Park Road, London
NW1 8XN
Tel: 0171 586 2960

Guinevere – *see* Antique Glass

Harvey Nicols, 67 Brompton Road,
London SW1X 7RG
Tel: 0171 235 5000

Liberty – *see* Quilts

Nina Campbell, 9 Walton Street
London SW3 2JD
Tel: 0171225 1011

Pierre Frey – *see* Contemporary
Fabrics

William Yeoward – *see* Contemporary
Glass

INDEX

LEFT The heavy ornate gold of this urn implies weightiness, whereas the blue and white design in the centre of the piece gives a sense of lightness, as if the scalloped gold were barely touching the porcelain.

to Chase

It's Saturday!!

I hop on my bike and go for a ride

through the woods,

past the reservoir,

along the stream,

through a covered bridge,

over the railroad tracks,
and past the cement factory.

I pedal up a giant hill.

At the top

I turn onto a trail
down into the valley.

I set sail...

through a sea of grass.

Then I hear something rustling.

A coyote appears just ahead of me.

For a short time we are running together.

When I stop, so does Coyote.
His eyes are wild, but I'm not afraid.

He lies down and scratches his back.

For a few fleeting moments we're
a part of each other's world.

And then, just like that, he dashes away.

"See you later, Coyote!"

He looks back at me,
then disappears into the woods.

I spend the rest of the day riding
around with my little brother.

I think about that coyote all day...
and all night, too.

The next morning I look for Coyote.
I look around my neighborhood, the woods,
the reservoir, the stream, the covered bridge,
the railroad tracks, and the cement factory.
I pedal to the top of the giant hill.
I sail down just like I did before.

This time Coyote doesn't join me.

I even go to the very last spot I saw him,
but he isn't there.

"Goodbye, Coyote."

Author's Note:

Coyote is a story about the morning I learned
of my brother Chase's unexpected passing.
I actually went on that bike ride — I saw and rode
with the coyote. When I returned home I learned
that Chase was gone. My wife Krista and I would
like to share this story to help children and their
families talk about loss. We will donate our proceeds
in Chase's memory, to the children of Sandy Hook.

~Lee Harper

Made in the USA
Charleston, SC
24 April 2014